A minister's guide

PLANNING A CHRISTIAN FUNERAL

W. A. POOVEY

AUGSBURG Publishing House • Minneapolis

PLANNING A CHRISTIAN FUNERAL

Copyright © 1978 Augsburg Publishing House

Library of Congress Catalog Card No. 78-52198

International Standard Book No. 0-8066-1668-7

Scripture quotations unless otherwise noted are from the Revised Standard Version of the Bible, copyright 1946, 1952, and 1971 by the Division of Christian Education of the National Council of Churches.

MANUFACTURED IN THE UNITED STATES OF AMERICA

Contents

Introduction

"In the midst of life. . . . " Every minister knows the rest of that quotation. The phone rings or there is a knock on the door. A child has died in the hospital. An accident on an icy road has snuffed out a family. A long period of suffering for a cancer patient and her friends has come to an end. Regardless of the circumstances, the rest of the quotation fits, "we are in death."

And the minister is faced with one of life's most difficult tasks, that of saying comforting words to those who mourn. Perhaps no responsibility in a parish causes such agony of spirit, such sense of failure as the funeral. Somehow every death brings with it frustration, a feeling of being beyond one's depth in the presence of the mystery of eternity. Most can sympathize with William A. Buege when he says:

> It would appear that death not only marks the end-limit of our lives but also the end-limit of what we can say. We still speak words about death, brave or despairful words, sympathetic or cold words, understanding or stupid words, but hardly meaningful words out of the understanding of personal experience and direct knowledge. We just don't know that it means to die and so we either try to live by ignoring death or we try to give

explanations that really explain nothing except our own folly.[1]

One of the perplexing problems for the preacher is the lack of time for careful preparation of funeral sermons. The harried minister can join with Everyman in the cry: "O Death, thou comest when I had thee least in mind." Most special occasions can be planned for. The minister knows when Christmas is to be celebrated. Congregational anniversaries, Lenten services, even Mother's Day have their places on the regular calendar. But death cannot be predicted. Often it occurs with no warning at all. Even if we know that someone is dying, the process may take a long time and sometimes it seems as if people purposely choose the most inconvenient time for their demise. Of course that isn't true, but the frustrated and busy minister can be forgiven for harboring such dark thoughts.

The purpose of this book is to render some help for the busy preacher. The first part of the book deals with the whole area of funerals. People are particularly sensitive when death occurs and it is easy to make a mistake and offend. Since death occurs only once for each individual, the preacher gets only one chance to do and to say the proper things. So there are suggestions here for ministering through the funeral. The suggestions and discussions arise out of seventeen years in the parish ministry and eighteen years of teaching preaching at Wartburg Seminary in Dubuque. You may not agree with all that is said but perhaps you will find some guidance that will make the task of dealing with death a little easier.

The second half of the book consists of funeral sermons written by twenty different ministers. Because the sermon must be prepared on short notice, the preacher must grab for ideas. He may have to be a borrower. While it is unwise for a minister to rely on others for ideas, the funeral is an exception. Here any help should be grasped. In the words of Kipling:

> When 'Omer smote 'is blooming lyre,
> He'd 'eard men sing by land and sea;
> An' what he thought 'e might require,
> 'E went an' took—the same as we!

So this book is intended to help the minister who faces the difficult task of preaching and officiating at a funeral. If the suggestions and the sermons make that task a little easier, the book will have achieved its purpose.

Note

1. *Preaching About Death.* Ed. by Alton M. Motter. (Philadelphia: Fortress, 1975), 6.

Part One

PLANNING
THE
FUNERAL

Why a Funeral?

A body lies on a hospital bed. A few moments ago this was a living human being. Blood flowed through arteries and veins. Air filled and then was emptied from lungs. Nerve impulses ran back and forth from the brain. Now all of this is over. Death has come. There is little outward change in the body. You might expect the lips to speak again, the head to move, the eyes to focus. But it is all over for this person. The body has become a useless, empty piece of matter.

What shall we do with this dead body? Call someone to haul it away and bury it before it pollutes the atmosphere? Burn it up in some kind of incinerator? It is no good to anyone anymore. The body is about to fulfill God's words in Genesis 3:19: "You are dust, and to dust you shall return."

Human beings have never been satisfied with such a casual ending to life. In every culture death has been surrounded with some form of ritual, some type of ceremony before the body was destroyed or abandoned. In a book entitled *Funeral Customs the World Over,* the authors say,

> There is no group, however primitive at the one ex-
> treme or civilized at the other, which left freely to itself
> and within its means does not dispose of the bodies of
> its members with ceremony. . . . It is natural, normal,
> reasonable. It satisfies deep universal urges.[1]

At times such ceremonies are performed out of fear.
Primitive people particularly cannot accept death as a
natural phenomenon. They believe that a ghost, a spirit
survives and rituals must be performed to appease the
ghost. As someone has said, people want to make sure
that the dead are happy and are far away from the
living.

Funeral ceremonies also are an act of love. Although
every human being beyond the age of infancy is aware
that every individual must die, that never makes it any
easier when death comes. In the words of Edgar N.
Jackson: "When the fabric of life has been tightly
woven together, the rending of the fabric is hard to
repair." People in every age have felt sorrow at the
death of someone close to them, for grief is not the
product of civilization but of our humanity. Human
beings have thus sought to perform some last act of
love, some action which becomes "the least I can do."

Whatever the reasons, funeral rites may vary but they
are part of the common instincts of human beings.
While most funerals today are conducted by the church,
the practice did not originate with Christianity. In fact,
there is no command in the New Testament for the
church to be involved in funerals at all. Jesus once told
a young man to let the dead bury their dead, which
would be a rather difficult task if taken literally. The
elaborate rituals which various churches have developed

in connection with the dead are man-made and have no direct biblical approval.

Indeed one may ask, "Why have funerals at all?" The Christian church believes in the resurrection. We believe that the one who has died will live again. We share with Paul the conviction that to depart and be with Christ is better than to remain in this imperfect world. Wouldn't it be better for the church to refuse to be involved in funerals? After all, our business is with the living, not the dead.

That is precisely why the church *is* involved in funerals. Our business is with the living! And death can be a terrible jolt to the faith of the survivors. All our fine Christian rhetoric seems empty when death comes. Scripture rightly calls death the last enemy of mankind. One of the most revealing books on this subject is *A Grief Observed* by C. S. Lewis, written after the death of his wife. Lewis tells how he had to struggle back to faith after his loss. He writes:

> Not that I am in much danger of ceasing to believe in God. The real danger is of coming to believe such dreadful things about Him. The conclusion I dread is not "So there's no God after all," but "So this is what God's really like. Deceive yourself no longer." [2]

But what can the funeral do for the living? Can a brief twenty-five-minute service actually be of any help in the traumatic experience of death, followed by grief and separation? Our question remains, Why the Funeral?

1. Funerals satisfy the need of people to do something for the dead. There is a sense of helplessness

when death approaches. Doctors are summoned. Medicine is administered. The physician is implored to do something, anything to restore this person to health or at least to keep him or her alive. So death represents frustration of our best efforts. A funeral then can provide an outlet for this frustration.

I once sat behind two women on a bus who were discussing the imminent death of a relative. The younger woman was busy criticizing all funeral practices and her logic was impeccable. The money would be better spent elsewhere. The ceremony wouldn't bring back the dead one. The relative hadn't always been very kind to the rest of the family, etc., etc. I had to agree with all she was saying. But she was totally wrong.

For funeral customs have their own logic. They help relieve the frustration of death. They help bridge the transition back to normal living. They help relieve guilt feelings of past failures. They are "the least we can do."

For this reason ministers should be careful how they advise a family at the time of death. There is a temptation to discourage people from spending too much money on the dead. The minister may want to keep the funeral as simple as possible with no flowers, no fancy casket, etc. We need to see that some funeral customs may be worth the cost in therapy for the mourners.

This does not mean that we approve all of the established funeral rituals in a community. But the time to teach people the right approach to such matters is long before preparations are required. Funeral customs should be discussed among Christians. People should be encouraged to make their plans and to write out instructions for the time when the inevitable occurs.

But lessons on this subject should not be given at the actual time of death. Funerals satisfy the needs of people to do something for the dead and we should be careful not to meddle in this.

2. Funerals help people accept the painful reality of death. Preachers often describe death as a temporary separation, a journey to another part of the universe. But there is a finality about death that belies such a comparison. Death means that in this world you will never see that person again. The chair in which he sat will not be occupied by him any more. The dress she wore with such grace will never be worn by her again. The toys your child played with will never be touched by his chubby hands again.

And this reality is hard to accept. It still seems that the dead one should come walking through the door again, that the voice you knew and loved should come floating out of the next room. Death is a hard thing to accept. I can remember that when my father died, I simply couldn't believe that death had occurred. The doctors had to be wrong. My father was going to get up out of that coffin and talk to me again. It was only when I saw his body lowered into the grave that I faced the truth.

A funeral then makes us face painful reality. It says, "This is the end. You may have pleasant memories to comfort you but you must face the future without the presence of the one who is gone." And it is well that the entire community recognize that death has occurred. This is why I believe that the traditional funeral is better than the so-called memorial service, wherever possible. To quote Jackson again:

A funeral without the body present is somewhat like a baptism or marriage by proxy, or a birthday celebration without the birthday child there. The ceremony can be carried out, but it lacks individual identity.[3]

Of course there are times when a memorial service is the only possibility, but the importance of facing up to the reality of death must not be overlooked.

3. A funeral provides a time and place for the release of emotions. Human beings are strange, especially civilized human beings. Somehow we have gotten the idea that there is something weak, something crude and unseemly about displaying emotions. A stiff upper lip is supposed to be the idea. Don't let the other person see how you feel or he may think you foolish. When death comes to someone close to us, this inhibiting attitude fights with our natural tendency to give way. Many people try to conquer their sorrow by pretending they feel no sorrow or that they are too strong to be defeated by death. And this simply makes the situation worse.

The church has added to this problem by hinting that mourning is wrong. The dead one has gone to a better place. He or she has triumphed over this life and we should rejoice in that triumph. Mourning then is evidence of a lack of faith, a selfishness that would begrudge the dead one his or her bliss. So the argument runs. And it is a false type of reasoning. Of course we are not to mourn as those who have no hope. But stoic resignation at death is unloving and unchristian. Martin Luther knew better than that. In his Letters of Spiritual Counsel he wrote:

> For God has not created us to be without feeling or to be like stones or sticks, but it is his will that we should mourn and bewail our dead. Otherwise it would appear that we had no love, particularly in the case of members of our own family.

A funeral serves as an acceptable place where the emotions connected with death can be adequately expressed. It provides a place and a time where even strong silent he-men can reveal that they are human and can weep without feeling foolish. Of course all the sobbers at funerals aren't necessarily displaying genuine feelings of grief. I remember feeling so sorry for a daughter who cried all during a funeral but the undertaker informed me later that she wouldn't step inside the funeral parlor until assured that she wasn't going to have to pay for the funeral. But even though some sadness may be feigned, a funeral does provide the opportunity for genuine emotions to be displayed without any sense of embarrassment. That is good.

4. A funeral provides community support for the bereaved. One of the sad features of modern living is that we are cut off from one another. We often find no time for the friendly word, the concerned touch for others. Even families are widely scattered and thus lose contact with one another. A funeral may serve to bridge that gap, at least in part. People gather, moved by common concern for those who have suffered loss. Family members are in touch with one another, even if only for a brief time. And this has value for mourners. Alvin Rogness, who has known tragic loss in his own family, writes: "Quite apart from anything you say,

your presence is a language of sorrow and love. And it may be the most eloquent language for the moment." [4]

However, this concern needs to be an on-going thing. Grief does not cease when a body is buried. The deeper suffering comes later. And those who suffer loss almost universally complain that they are quickly forgotten. The words of sympathy are not translated into action. Loneliness and often bitterness set in. Both clergy and laity need to remember to follow through on their good intentions and concern. So a funeral provides an opportunity. But it is not the complete answer to grief.

5. A funeral allows the church to proclaim its most significant doctrine — the resurrection. Christianity began as a death-conquering religion. The apostles and their followers announced to a despairing world that there was hope. Death had been conquered. Jesus Christ had risen and he was the first fruits of resurrection. It is hard for us to recapture the excitement in the words of Jesus to Martha:

> I am the resurrection and the life; he who believes in me, though he die, yet shall he live and whoever lives and believes in me shall never die.

Bishop Pike put the Christian message very succinctly in his book *The Next Day:*

> Christianity offers us no escape from death, no way of hiding from it. The secret is this; the Christian Church, the Christian faith invites you to die now. And if you die now you'll never have to die again, in any real sense, in any ultimately disastrous sense.[5]

Of course this is a message that can be proclaimed

every Sunday. Each Sunday is a reminder to Christians that Christ has risen. Yet like Martha we all feel the message of the resurrection most strongly when we are in the presence of death. I remember preaching about the resurrection at the funeral of a faithful member and being told by her daughter afterwards, "I never knew death was like that." I think I had been emphasizing that message every Sunday and that she had been listening. But the presence of death clears the mind. At a funeral the ultimate comfort and triumph of the gospel can be proclaimed in ringing terms.

Why do we have funerals? Why does the church involve itself in this matter? For all the above reasons and for many others, I suppose. But perhaps the important thing is that we *have* funerals. The Christian minister has a duty and an opportunity here. Conducting funerals is an important part of the work of every parish pastor. Planning a Christian funeral is not an easy task, particularly in the time available. The next three chapters may help. But it is of paramount importance that we approach the funeral with the realization that here is a unique chance to present the message of the gospel to those who mourn.

Notes

1. R. W. Habenstein and William M. Lamers, *Funeral Customs the World Over.* (Bulfin Printers, 1960), 757.
2. C. S. Lewis, *A Grief Observed.* (Greenwich, Conn.: Seabury Press, 1963), 9.
3. Edgar N. Jackson, *For the Living.* (New York: Channel Press, 1963), 52-53.
4. Alvin N. Rogness, *Appointment with Death.* (New York: Nelson, 1972), 66.
5. James Albert Pike, *The Next Day.* (Garden City, N.Y.: Doubleday, 1957), pp. 150-151.

The Service

The telephone in the parsonage rings. It is the local undertaker, informing you that Mrs. Pilgrim has died and the family wishes you to conduct the funeral on Friday at 2 P.M. Or it may be a call from the hospital saying that Mr. Wilson has passed away after suffering a severe heart attack. Or that the newborn Jones baby hasn't survived.

Every pastor receives such calls and dreads them. Preparing for another funeral isn't a pleasant prospect. Often it means the loss of an important and useful member of the church. Always it involves an emotional and intellectual drain on the minister. And if the calls come too frequently, fellow clergy will jokingly inform you that you have a dying congregation. But funerals offer unusual opportunities to be of service to people in a dark hour. Many have had their hearts touched and their faith strengthened by a properly conducted funeral. And some have been driven away from the church because of calloused or clumsy efforts by ministers at the time of death. *A funeral service is important.* It should be Christian and helpful. A few guidelines may be useful.

1. THE PREPARATION. Every professional faces the danger of becoming perfunctory, of dealing with human beings as numbers, not as living persons. Doctors, lawyers, and social workers have this problem and the clergy are not exempt. Robert W. Bailey writes:

> A minister can conduct a number of funerals a year and never be involved emotionally. In order to stand the strain of constantly associating with the bereaved, he may put his emotions in neutral and sustain only a superficial relationship.[1]

Funerals can be burdensome. The time is often inconvenient. The family involved may not have shown much interest in the church. The mood of the preacher may be all out of harmony with death. The result may be a routine performance.

But this is a special funeral to the family. Someone has died, someone who was loved or who at least will be missed. The old saying is "Misery loves company." The reverse of this is that misery never appreciates coldness or the feeling of being ignored. So the wise minister seeks to understand and to share the grief of the family. They should be visited if possible and consulted about such things as the service, favorite hymns, and scripture passages. Usually they will say, "You take care of it, pastor," but they need to feel that their interests are considered. The concerned minister is the helpful and loved one.

2. THE PLACE. Andrew W. Blackwood in his book *The Funeral* published in 1942 declared that the logical place for many funerals is the home. Today the home has ceased to be a very viable option. Most services

are conducted either in the church or in the funeral parlor. The church is generally favored by ministers, at least for church members. It is easy to see why. The church has been the center of the individual's religious life. Here he or she was baptized and received communion. In the church the deceased had heard the word of God Sunday after Sunday. Moreover the church displays the symbols of worship, the cross, the altar, the windows and hangings. The tools of worship including the organ and the hymnals are available.

There are some objections, of course. A handful of mourners in a building that seats 500 to 1000 worshipers can seem rather pathetic and upsetting. Church pews were never noted for their comfort and elderly mourners may have their difficulties. Narrow aisles and steep steps add to the problems. I once knew a funeral director who refused to conduct a funeral in a certain church because the outside steps were too steep to carry a coffin up and down safely.

The funeral parlor has its pluses and minuses too. Such places are built for the special purpose of conducting funerals. They have all the conveniences needed. They can handle efficiently flowers, funeral cars, the coffin, etc. At the same time such parlors are only pseudo-churches, lacking any real religious associations. There is something necessarily commercial about the enterprise.

The decision as to place should be left to the family. Many churches have rules about allowing only church members to be buried from the church building. This seems rather foolish. A funeral offers a rare evangelistic opportunity, a chance to preach the gospel to people who may never hear it otherwise. Why run the risk of offending people by refusing to let them hold the service in the church? But the tendency today is to hold more and more services in the funeral parlor so perhaps the question of place isn't too important.

3. THE SERVICE. A funeral service conducted by a Christian minister is a *Christian* service. The entire worship must witness faithfully to the message which the church preaches every Sunday. Christians believe in Jesus Christ as Savior. They believe in life beyond the grave. They believe in God's love and forgiveness. These things need to be reflected in a funeral service. This is not a time for eulogizing the dead or for changing the rules and putting everybody comfortably in heaven. The message of the church is the same under all circumstances.

That doesn't mean that we are called upon to be judges in this world. The minister may have his suspicions about the future home of the deceased. But no one has appointed us to do God's business of deciding the fate of each human being. There is some judgment of course in the choosing of Scripture and prayer at a funeral. Wisdom must dictate such choices, but we must always be careful not to give offense. Remember how Laertes in *Hamlet* demanded: "What ceremony else?" and was terribly upset to find that the funeral rites had been curtailed because Ophelia had been judged a suicide.

The real answer to the problem of judging is that the funeral service is for the living. The hymns, the readings, the liturgy and the sermon are all aimed at the people who are present. Death has come for one but life remains for many. The minister must seek to point them away from sorrow to the one who said, "Blessed are they that mourn, for they shall be comforted." A funeral may be a time to thank God for his blessings, a time to lament the loss that comes in death, a time to puzzle at the strangeness of life, but it is above all a time to point to the Christ who suffered death to bring us life.

4. THE ELEMENTS OF WORSHIP. The following are usually included in a Christian funeral: Scripture; music; liturgy, including prayers; a sermon; and perhaps an obituary. Let's look at each of these ingredients.

a. Scripture. The Bible still speaks to people today, particularly in moments of deep emotion. No funeral service is complete without the reading of some Scripture. Of course biblical passages weren't designed with funerals in mind any more than they were written to provide preachers with sermon texts. So the preacher must make a careful selection. Sometimes a passage has acquired a special meaning because it was a favorite of the deceased or of some member of the family. But one thing is important—the meaning should be clear without any explanation. The Psalms contain beautiful passages for reading aloud. Some of the clear passages from Revelation are useful as are the discourses of Jesus in the Gospel of John. At times a medley of short passages may bring comfort and awaken memory.

Some clergy like to augment the service with modern readings, usually poetry or prose passages dealing with death. There is nothing wrong with such readings if tastefully chosen, but much literature in this field is hopelessly sentimental and void of any true Christian meaning. The Victorian period bequeathed us a lot of sloppy material and such stuff should be avoided. But if a selection is in harmony with the occasion, it may be very useful. Devout writers may still write worthwhile truth even though the canon of Scripture was closed long ago.

b. Music. Luther said, "Music is the noblest gift of God, next to theology." History agrees with his verdict, for Lutheran hymns did as much to spread the Reformation as did sermons and writings on theological points. In fact music and religion have always been partners, perhaps because both have deep emotional appeal. But it is precisely because of this emotional connection that music used at a funeral should be selected carefully. For people are emotionally disturbed at the time of death and a sentimental hymn can provoke floods of tears. This may not be a bad thing, but often it comes close to playing with people's feelings.

The hymnals of most congregations contain great songs of praise to God and these are most fitting for a funeral service. "Praise to the Lord, the Almighty," "Holy, holy, holy," "Jerusalem the Golden" and many similar hymns express the Christian attitude toward God, even in time of sorrow. If possible the songs should be sung by the congregation unless the group is too small. The New Testament speaks of songs sung in heaven by the redeemed. There is something inspiring about our singing songs here too when others depart for the next world.

c. Liturgy. Churches that use a liturgical service will not find it strange to have some liturgical responses as part of a funeral service. This material must be kept simple because there are always strangers at a funeral and a complicated liturgy can prove a barrier, particularly since there is no time to practice the liturgical responses.

Of course there is no need for formal ritual if a simple service is preferred. Scripture readings, prayers and a short sermon can suffice. This may even be preferable if the congregation is small or is composed of people who are unfamiliar with the use of formal liturgy. The pastor must play this by ear.

The ritual at the grave is of necessity simple and brief. The old custom of throwing dirt or dust into an open grave isn't to my liking but there are places where this custom is so firmly established that one pastor had to go out the next day and perform this rite because the family was not satisfied that their relative had been properly buried. Graveside committal services are declining because of the increase in cremation, memorial services and the donation of the body to medical science. In such instances of course the service is completed at the church or funeral parlor.

d. The sermon. This portion of the service will be discussed in the next chapter.

e. The obituary. The reading of a formal obituary has fallen into disuse in many areas of the church. Newspapers now publish obituary material and often the undertaker prepares a printed program listing vital facts about the deceased. There is nothing right or wrong about obituaries. Such a reading does add a personal note to the service, and if families desire it, the minister should agree. Only, *get it right*. Just recently a correction appeared in a local newspaper, apologizing for listing someone as the stepsister of the deceased when she was in fact a half sister. Of such slips are offended feelings made.

As these words are being written the TV is reporting the death of Hubert Humphrey, former vice-president of the United States. Humphrey reportedly told his clergyman a short time before his death that he didn't want a eulogy at his funeral but a celebration. Good for him! Whenever it is possible, that note should be sounded. Even in the case of sudden and tragic death we can celebrate Christ's victory, which gives us cause for hope. Death is a tragedy and we should not try to deny the fact but the gospel is good news, even in time of death. Especially in time of death!

Note

1. Robert Bailey, *The Minister and Grief*. (New York: Hawthorn, 1976), 31.

The Sermon

Ministers often grow enthusiastic about various phases of their work. Some love to preach. Sunday morning when they step into the pulpit, they are in their glory. Others love the rituals of the church and find joy in planning and participating in a colorful worship service. Some love to work with youth, others prefer to minister to the elderly. But no one has ever heard a minister say, "I love to preach funeral sermons." It is not hard to understand why this should be an unpopular activity. Lack of time for adequate preparation is a problem. The peculiar and unpredictable mood of the mourners is a problem. The absence of a clear picture of life beyond death in the Scriptures is a problem. But the most difficult barrier is the emotional one. If you do not know the family, it is hard to appreciate their grief. But if the person who has died is well known to you and the mourners are close friends, that is even worse. Ministers feel that they dare not break down and weep at funerals. They are to help others bear the pain of separation, but if the preacher's heart is heavy, it is not easy to say the things that should be said.

Some deal with this problem by omitting the funeral sermon entirely. Liturgical responses, prayers and hymns form the funeral service for many clergy. But there are difficulties about such a service. Unless you rigidly exclude sermons in every case, even when an important or faithful member dies, people will feel that you discriminate. Also there is a certain stiffness, a sense of the impersonal about a service with no funeral message for it is in the sermon that the ritual becomes particular and personal. In addition, the funeral address can be a means of bringing the gospel to people who may never be present at a Sunday morning service. A funeral gives the minister the opportunity to talk about death in a natural setting. So, despite the problems, funeral sermons can serve a worthwhile purpose and the Christian church would be foolish to abandon them.

But what should a funeral sermon be like? How does it differ from the regular message delivered on Sunday morning? No hard and fast rules can be laid down, for every funeral is different and every minister has his or her special way of approaching the homiletical task. There are, however, some general observations and some lines of approach that can be pointed out. Let's take a look at a few of them.

1. *A funeral sermon should be biblical.* This does not mean that the preacher must quote a lot of Scripture during his sermon or engage in exegetical explanations to the congregation. But as previously mentioned, the Bible does not give too clear a picture of the nature of eternity or of life after death. We get some brief glimpses now and then but the whole plan is not laid out before us.

Probably the biblical reticence is a blessing. But it is also a temptation for preachers to rush in and flesh out the details for those who mourn. And such efforts can be sadly misleading.

One of the commonest temptations is to insist that the spirit of the departed is with us. "He knows what we are doing today." "She appreciates all these beautiful flowers." Such messages are comforting for mourners. The success of mediums and spiritualists depends on this longing to be close to the departed. But there is no biblical warrant for such a view. *Christ* has promised to be with us always but there is no such assurance about our loved ones. The preacher is also tempted to engage in vivid descriptions of heaven and the reunion with loved ones. "Joe is up there now with grandpa and grandma. What a great reunion." So the story goes. But we have no such picture given to us in the Scriptures. Even with the best of motives, the preacher should not play fast and loose with the Bible.

Whether a funeral sermon should have a text or not depends on the preacher. The sermons in the second part of this book do have texts and although the preachers were not assigned passages, there is no duplication. The Bible is full of material which is useful at the time of death. Any passage that speaks of God's care, his concern and love for his people is usable as a funeral text. Of course there are favorites like the 23rd and the 90th psalms, Jesus' words to Martha at the death of Lazarus, John 11:25, 26, Paul's great assurance in Romans 8:35-39 that nothing can separate us from God's love, and some of the magnificent pictures in Revelation. But the minister who knows his Bible should have no difficulty with choosing a text. In the case of a funeral sermon it may be wiser to select the particular approach that you want to make and then choose a text that fits.

2. *A funeral sermon should be positive.* People at a funeral have already had enough gloom. They don't need to hear doleful words from the pulpit. I once had a professor who loved to say, "This is a weary wicked world and few of us get out of it alive." That's well and good for a classroom lecture but it isn't the kind of message needed at a funeral. Often the preacher is tempted to talk too much about sin which infects all of us and brings us to death, but this isn't much help at a funeral. A friend of mine preached a sermon which he thought was orthodox and fitting at death. It had the typical three-part outline.

1. This man was a sinner.

2. This man was a redeemed sinner.

3. This man will be a resurrected sinner.

It looks so nice on paper. No one would criticize its doctrinal purity. But the family was unhappy with what was said. "Why bring that up at a funeral?" they complained and their attitude was understandable. A positive approach to the congregation, even if not to the corpse, is important.

3. *A funeral sermon should be interesting.* That sounds strange. People shouldn't need to be entertained at a funeral. But the human attention span is short at

best and the minds of mourners are filled with many divergent thoughts. A dull discourse will be useless and worse than that. So the wise preacher uses a lot of illustrative material in the sermon. Stories, poems, hymn verses, Scripture passages, and personal experiences with the deceased can all be of help in holding the attention of the congregation. Of course this is no time for radical or strange innovations. Several years ago a student preached a funeral sermon in one of my classes and used slides and recorded music during the sermon. It was a bold try but I wouldn't recommend it. But notice the sermons reproduced in this book. Several of them are outstanding for their use of illustrative material. This helps the reader and even more the hearer of the message.

4. *A funeral sermon should be simple.* In other words, the message should be quickly grasped, for mourners are not in the mood for wrestling with theological niceties. There are times on Sunday when it is proper to ask the congregation to do some heavy thinking. My old teacher, Paul Scherer, when told that he was preaching over people's heads once said, "Let them lift their heads a little." Such an attitude may be justified at times. There are depths to Christian faith and as the writer of Hebrews tells us, we can't keep going over the simple things. But a funeral is no place for an involved discourse. Paul's reasoning in 1 Corinthians 15 about a physical body and a spiritual body may form the basis of a Sunday morning sermon. The difference between immortality of the soul and resurrection of the body may require explanation. But not at a funeral. Peo-

ple are too heavily involved in grief. And there may be many present who are not well-versed in Christianity. The funeral sermon should be simple.

5. *A funeral sermon should be short.* In these days when we barely get seated before the preacher says amen, it should not be necessary to mention this point. If the preacher is going to say anything worthwhile, it will take some time to do so. Nevertheless, funeral sermons should be brief and to the point. Local customs differ, of course, and some people feel cheated if the message is too brief, but a funeral is a strain on everyone and the preacher should not tire out his audience.

6. *A funeral sermon should be delivered in understandable tones.* Modern public address systems have eliminated many of the troubles clergy once had being heard. The microphone makes it possible for the minister to speak naturally to the congregation, and this is a real blessing. No one likes to be yelled at, especially at a funeral. But the difficulty lies in the other direction. The preacher usually wants to be soothing and comforting with his message. The speaker wants to be the good friend who pours advice into the ears of those who need help. And this leads to complaints that the message can't be heard. Often there are elderly people present at funerals, people who have trouble hearing. And funeral parlors may have acoustics that are strange to the pastor. The result can be disastrous. People strain to hear for a moment and then just sit back and wait for the service to end. The conversational tone style of delivery is a great step forward for Sunday morning but

it has a built-in booby trap for the funeral sermon. The minister needs to take care that he keeps his volume loud enough to be heard by the congregation.

But what do we say at funerals? Are there any guidelines for the preacher? There are at least four major motifs in the Bible regarding death, and funeral sermons generally make use of one of them. They are: death itself, hope for the future, a challenge to the living, and the comfort of memories. Let's look at each in more detail.

a. Emphasis on death. Death is a natural subject to discuss in a funeral sermon since it is on everyone's mind. The preacher can at least use this as the starting point, although the subject is so broad that it must be narrowed for an effective sermon. One of the difficulties is that we talk so little about death that one funeral sermon can only touch the surface. I remember having to help bury a young girl who had been drowned in a boating accident. As I stepped into the pulpit, where I was filling in for the regular pastor, the thought flashed in my mind: "If these people have not heard anything about death before from this pulpit, I can't do much in this one short sermon." Pastors ought to include sermons about death in their regular preaching schedule. The topic should be discussed in Bible classes and in various group meetings. Fortunately we seem to be recovering from our head-in-the-sand attitude about death. But there are many aspects of death and the circumstances of the funeral will determine what our approach should be.

Someone has defined a human being as an animal

that knows it's going to die. The inevitability of death is one approach and a good one, particularly when the service is being conducted for an unchurched or unfamiliar individual. A funeral is a reminder that what has happened to one will happen to us all. One is reminded of that long list of names in Genesis 5 with the refrain: "And he died. And he died." Only Enoch interrupts that melancholy phrase. This stress on inevitability removes the idea of divine revenge against an individual. The preacher should avoid the statement: "This is God's will." Death is a universal part of living and the preacher may move on to thoughts of preparing for the inevitable day when each one faces death. At least this is a good starting point.

A number of years ago *Reader's Digest* published an article entitled "Sudden Death." The writer was referring to auto accidents on the highways but the title is a motif for many funerals. Human beings are very tough at times and can withstand almost unbelievable hardships. But we are also fragile creatures and death can come with amazing swiftness. The words of the committal service—in the midst of life we are in death—fit many funerals. When sudden death has occurred, this may be the major motif of the sermon. The shock of seeing a man yesterday and finding he is dead today focuses our mind strikingly on our own mortality. Sudden death is strangely like the Second Coming as described in Scripture and the biblical warnings to be ready, to be prepared, to redeem the time, all fit under this heading. The sermon may reflect on this truth.

Death is also the clearest proof of the imperfection of this life. There was a time when most people lived short and unhappy lives and thought of this world only as a vale of tears. Life is different today and many settle down comfortably to enjoy the good things here. This is not wrong, but it is only part of the picture. Death reminds us that this world is not as God intended it to be. Pain and grief shake us out of our complacency. Sirach writes in *The Apocrypha:*

> O death how bitter is the remembrance of thee to a man that liveth at rest in his possessions, to a man that hath nothing to vex him, and that hath prosperity in all things; yea, unto him that is yet able to receive meat.

Death then teaches us to see life in its entirety—this life and the world beyond. It makes us realize that there will be no real peace for human beings until the last enemy of mankind has been destroyed. This can be a powerful preaching motif.

But of course sometimes death is not enemy but a friend. It may bring release from pain and suffering and may move the survivors to say, "Thank God she's at rest." The Bible does speak of a rest for the children of God. Somehow the human body wears out and even more tragically the mind dims for some people. When this occurs it is not wrong to talk about God "taking this one home." But even when there is relief in death we must not forget that there is still separation, and sadness that someone had to suffer so. But where it fits, the idea of death as a rest may be a proper preaching approach.

b. The Christian hope. There is no sadder word in the English language than *hopeless.* Human beings can face any situation if there is hope. Fortunately, Christians facing the reality of death still have a blessed hope. We believe that the one who has died will live again and that God has promised eternal life for those who put their trust in him. The details are not clear. The question of an interim existence between death and the resurrection is a subject for theological debate. But the promise of resurrection and life everlasting is repeated every Sunday in most Christian churches. This truth is deeply rooted in the New Testament and it is the central message of the preacher at the death of a Christian, for this is our hope.

Of course, belief in the survival of the dead is found among most religions and even among those who profess no formal faith. So the sermon should always make plain the source of our hope. Christian hope is based on two things—the promise of God and the resurrection of Jesus Christ. We do not need to talk about man's longing for life to continue, or about the ultimate worth of a human being. We have God's promise and that should be enough. For the recurring message of the Old and New Testaments is that God keeps his word. He does what he promises and we can trust him.

The resurrection of Jesus is God's stamp of approval to all this. Jesus is the first fruits, the firstborn among the dead. Others will follow. A funeral sermon should not be used as a time to "prove" Christ's resurrection. Rather the resurrection is an example of what will happen to the one who has died. Of course this message of resurrection may not be the fitting one for every funeral but it is the central biblical truth about death and should be the center of the sermon wherever possible.

c. A challenge to the living. It may seem strange to talk about life in the presence of a corpse but the people who attend a funeral are going to go out of the church or funeral parlor and take up their normal way of living again. Even the close members of the family who may feel that life is over for them will have to take up life's routine again. Does this death say anything to them about how life should be lived? The sermon may concern itself with this question.

People at funerals are often filled with guilt. The kind words that they meant to say to the deceased are useless now. The plans that they had for the future have been cancelled. Too late, too late. There is no point in stressing this guilt in the sermon, but death does remind us to redeem the time, to take action toward others while we may. The kindest thing we can do for the dead is to show more love and concern for the living. The sermon can convey this challenge to the listeners.

But people who mourn also need comfort for the days ahead. Jesus promised that those who mourn will be comforted but we must know how to stress this point. Sometimes ministers like to say that time will heal the hurt, and while this is true, it isn't much comfort to tell people they will forget about their sorrow. Note that "shall be comforted" is a future passive. Comfort comes from outside us, from God and from faithful friends. Moreover there is no time limit set. No one should expect immediate help. Sometimes the hurt lingers for years but those who mourn should be encouraged to look to God and await his good time. This can be a helpful message at a funeral.

d. The comfort of memories. A death occurs at a moment in time. At a funeral it seems the only reality for those who mourn, but often a whole lifetime has gone before. People treasure memories and the minister should encourage people to see the whole life, not just the tragic moment. Reminding people of the past may make the present more bitter for a little while but in the long run pleasant memories have a way of over-shadowing some of the gloom of death. The sermon may remind the congregation to see the whole life of the deceased, not just the agony of the present or the immediate past.

In addition, a funeral is a time for reminding our-serves of what remains behind. What imprint has the deceased made on the lives of others? Possessions have a way of disappearing but the memories of deeds of kindness and love remain. In the judgment scene in Matthew the people on the right have left memories of feeding the hungry, caring for the unclothed, etc. Revelation tells us that the works of those who die in the Lord follow them. These truths also may be a part of the funeral sermon. We are not to eulogize the dead but it would be cruel to overlook such pleasant memories. An emphasis like this carries with it the challenge of what will remain behind when death comes to us. Memories can be the central motif of a funeral meditation.

In every type of activity there are problem cases, difficult tasks that challenge and worry us. And while all funeral sermons are hard to compose, there are several that pose particular difficulties. Let's take a quick look at several of them.

i. The unchurched. Preachers are often accused of putting everyone in heaven at a funeral. One can understand the feeling of an abused wife who heard the minister extolling her dead husband. She told one of her children: "Step over there to the casket and see if that's your daddy he's talking about." It *is* difficult to say the correct things when the corpse is not known to have been a Christian, particularly when other members of the family have been faithful church members. The simplest way to deal with this is to speak to the congregation about death and its meaning to us or to talk about the place where we can find comfort. The preacher is not the judge of the dead and he is not called on to wound the living. Even a scoundrel may have some people who mourn his passing. Some of the areas of Christian truth listed above will serve for a funeral sermon for the unchurched.

ii. Death of a child. This is always a difficult sermon to prepare. It seems so tragic and wasteful that a child comes into this world, lives only a short time and then is gone. And the grief is always deep on such an occasion. Fortunately there are adequate preaching helps available. Jesus' love for children can be used to bring assurance that God is not punishing anyone through such a death. The message that here we see through a glass darkly can be stressed. The preacher should make no effort to explain why this death has occurred. We are not appointed to justify God or to explain how this universe is run.

Preachers are tempted to put a strong stress on Baptism at the funeral of a child. This is a natural impulse for those who believe in the efficacy of infant Baptism but there is a stumbling block. If we pitch the message too strong, we are faced with the question of the child who dies unbaptized. The preacher's words may come back to haunt him when a small child dies suddenly before it has been baptized. It is better to emphasize God's love, of which Baptism is an example. It is never easy to preach at the death of a child but Scripture does provide some comfort.

iii. The suicide. There have been times in the history of the church when suicide was considered an unforgiveable sin since there was no time for repentance. Fortunately we have been delivered from that kind of theology. But suicide always faces the preacher with the question of what to say. There is a fine sermon for a suicide in the second part of this book and it deserves careful study. As a general rule it is wise to refuse to sit in judgment over anyone and to leave the deceased in the hands of a merciful and forgiving God. Having done that, the preacher may proceed to speak to the living about God's care and love for us. Any statements about suicide should be left to the morning sermon or to a study group. Such a discussion should not be a part of a funeral sermon.

This chapter began with the statement that no one likes to preach funeral sermons. Yet perhaps it is at death that our Christian gospel can be seen most clearly. Thank God we have something to say when death comes. We cannot abolish the tragedy but we can place alongside it the hope and promise of the resurrection. Preaching for funerals is difficult. But it is also a rewarding task!

The Congregation

Who attends funerals today? That question is important for the preacher. For like any speaker or public performer, the minister must be concerned about his audience. If the message doesn't meet the needs of those who are present, it is a failure no matter how thoughtfully it has been prepared or how well it has been presented. Who are those who are being addressed? Of course, the number of people in attendance varies from funeral to funeral. But in general we can divide the congregation in attendance into two groups—members of the family, and others. Let's take a look at each segment of the congregation because they do not necessarily have the same needs or expectations at a funeral.

1. THE FAMILY. The definition of a family grows narrower these days. Once the family included, as in *H.M.S. Pinafore*, "His sisters and his cousins whom he reckons up by dozens, and his aunts." Today the family circle is smaller and the members are more widely scattered than in the past. But modern air travel makes it possible for relatives to fly in, attend a funeral and return home the same day. So probably the immediate

family is as well-represented at modern funerals as it ever was.

The service, and especially the sermon, needs to include recognition of the special grief of the family. This is not a time for talking about death in general but about the death of an individual who was bound to the mourners by special ties of blood. As previously indicated, the sermon should not be a eulogy of the dead but the preacher needs to recognize that a special event has called the congregation together. Sometimes this fact is overlooked. When grading funeral sermons written by students, I often had to write across the paper, "Who died?" The language was so general that the sermon would have fitted anybody. Students can be forgiven this error but the officiating clergyman should never make the same mistake. The sermon which fits everybody is not suitable for anyone.

Sometimes the minister must admit: "I did not personally know the one who died." Even then the special interest that members of the family had in the one who has died should be acknowledged. If the preacher has been given some personal material about the individual, a reference to this will help make the service fit this particular family and no other.

But the preacher dare not expect too much from a funeral sermon. It will not provide all the comfort that is needed at the time of death. Nature has fortunately provided human beings with a kind of anesthetic, a state of shock in the face of death. The full reality comes when people go home to a house where someone is now missing. Joyce Phipps talks about this feeling in her book *Death's Single Privacy* (Seabury).

Death as I met it was pain. . . . A belief in the immortality of the soul did not erase the loneliness I felt and still feel when I walk into the house. When I open the door, there may be a cat or two, but there is no Bob. And when I wake in the middle of the night, my bed half-empty, cerebral meditations on the resurrection and the life to come remain cerebral (p. 116).

So the comforting words of the sermon and the service may not reach the people who are most immediately affected by the tragedy. People's minds are awhirl at the time of a funeral. Their bodies may be exhausted from nervous and physical strain. The most eloquent address may come to them as something that they hear and yet do not hear. Often people ask for a copy of the funeral address and it is wise to have a copy or a tape available. Such requests may be an evidence that the mourners have heard something that they wanted to understand but were not in a position to grasp at the moment. Edward D. Dobihel Jr. writes in *Death and Ministry* (Seabury):

Too many seminarians and clergy quote too soon such scriptural statements as "Death is swallowed up in victory. O death, where is thy victory? O death where is thy sting?" They seem to have in this statement, followed by the message of Christ's triumph, a solid foundation, a proclamation of hope, and yet when it comes from an abstract formulation it collapses in the face of the actual situation of the suffering of the dying, or of angry, depressed and miserable mourners (p. 136).

The great danger is that the minister in talking to the mourners will hold out to them such a high standard of Christianity that he will create guilt feelings because they find themselves unable to measure up. It is so easy to say, "She is safe with Jesus. Let us rejoice in her victory." Or, "God loves little children and so you can rejoice even in your sorrow." But the minister must try to put himself or herself in place of the mourners. Death looks different when we think that it might have been our wife, our child. That doesn't mean that we should not proclaim the great comforting truths of the gospel. It does mean that it may take time for the truths to sink in. Just as the Sunday morning sermon doesn't produce immediate repentance and reformation in the lives of all hearers, so the funeral sermon and service take time to do their work. We must sow the seed and wait for the harvest.

2. THE OTHERS. The term "others" isn't a very descriptive term but it is the only one that covers the wide diversity of people at a funeral. There may be distant relatives present who have come out of a sense of duty or who want to see Cousin Allan from California for a few minutes. There are friends and neighbors who come because they think it is expected of them. There may be people present who worked with the deceased or who were business acquaintances. One is reminded of the characters in *A Christmas Carol* who promise to attend Scrooge's funeral in the imaginary scene of the future.

> "It's likely to be a very cheap funeral," said the same speaker; "for upon my life I don't know of anybody to go to it. Suppose we make up a party and volunteer."
> "I don't mind going if lunch is provided," observed

the gentleman with the excrescence on his nose. "But I
must be fed, if I make one."

There was a time when the entire community turned out
for a funeral. That day is over. But there are always
people present who are not the chief mourners at such
a service.

All too often these "others" are ignored at a funeral
service. In an effort to bring comfort to the family, the
minister addresses his entire message to the wife or
husband who is bereaved and the rest are simply allowed to listen in. And this is a shame, for a funeral
offers the preacher a rare opportunity to speak to an
entire group about a very touchy subject.

Everyone is aware of how hard modern people try to
avoid the subject of death. We avoid the word in our
speech. We whisk the dead from the hospital to the
funeral parlor where the body is so carefully treated
that people look better in death than they have for the
past twenty years. Yet no one can ignore death at a
funeral. Members of a congregation are bound to think:
"It might be me, lying there instead of Joe or Martha."
Harry S. Olin says, "The inevitability of personal death
becomes clearer during personal bereavement." The
minister thus has an ideal audience at a funeral, a congregation with an object lesson before them.

Under the circumstances it is foolish and wrong to
miss such a chance for bringing to people the importance of this life and the necessity to prepare for death
now. There is an evangelistic opportunity at the time of
a funeral. I do not mean that the preacher should be
brazen in an effort to make people face up to life. I

once heard of a preacher who had an altar call as a part of a funeral service. That's too much of the eager beaver. But a funeral is a God-given opportunity to reach people with the message of the gospel. The "others" should be seriously considered when preparing the funeral service and the message.

Of course no one can say that all of those present at a funeral will be in church next Sunday. Many are already church members. Some may be stirred for the moment and then lapse back into their normal routines. Some may listen politely and yet not hear a word that was said. But people have been won for God at funerals. People have been renewed in mind and spirit by well-chosen words at the time of death. The wise minister will keep in mind the "others" when preparing a funeral address.

Because of the opportunity to preach the gospel, ministers are foolish to refuse a funeral unless the family makes impossible demands. Some pastors have refused to officiate unless the person is a member of the local congregation. That is an easy way to avoid the difficult funeral where you do not know anything about the one who has died. But it means that the preacher loses an opportunity to witness for Christ. And that is too bad.

The joy and despair of all religious work is that unknown factor, that cannot be predicted or understood. The word may touch the heart of a mourner and help heal a terrible hurt. On the other hand the message may fall flat, doing nothing for anyone. Someone who came to the funeral simply out of a sense of duty may be shaken by what he hears or sees. There is no way to tell about such things. But the minister in preparing the service and the sermon must visualize the congregation. He must see the mourners and the others in his mind's eye. Having done that, the rest must be left in God's hands. He is the only one who knows what happens when we officiate at a funeral. And he isn't telling.

Part Two

FUNERAL
SERMONS

THE PREACHER — Richard A. Anderson was born in Osage, Iowa. He is a graduate of St. Olaf College and Wartburg Seminary and has done graduate work at the University of Michigan School of Social Work. He has served as pastor of the Artesian Parish, Artesian, South Dakota and at present is pastor of St. George Lutheran Church, Brighton, Michigan.

THE OCCASION—The sermon was preached at the funeral of a forty-three-year old wife and mother of three children. The woman died of cancer.

THE COMMENTS—Funeral sermons need to be clear and simple in structure. The preacher here is concise in the presentation of theme and parts so that the mourners should have no difficulty in following the message. The sermon is also effective in that it speaks directly to the needs of those present.

The Comfort
of the Cross

Therefore, since we are justified by faith, we have peace with God through our Lord Jesus Christ. Through him we have obtained access to this grace in which we stand, and we rejoice in our hope of sharing the glory of God. Romans 5:1-2

Friends in Christ. The symbol of the cross for Christians of all ages means Christ's victory over sin, death, and the devil. We stand in that assurance today as we gather to give glory to God for his goodness, and to remember a wife, mother, and a good friend. Victory has been won for her and for us, and the cross of Christ continues to speak to our immediate need. For our meditation today consider "The Comfort of the Cross."

The comfort of the cross promises us peace with God even at a time when we are in deep sorrow and distress. Ours is a time when outward peace is shattered by the separation of a loved one. Ours is a time when all inward peace is thrown into turmoil and conflict because a loving wife and mother has suddenly been taken from our midst. We seek to restore peace, but oftentimes we seek to do so through our own inner strengths and resources. We are not alone in this search for peace; man throughout time has sought peace by bargaining or blaming God. We know that Job once cried out to God, "I am not at ease, nor am I quiet; I have no rest; but trouble comes" (Job 3:26). He could not grasp the tragedy in his life, nor could he find peace with God. The hectic pace of modern life does not seem to offer us peaceful solutions to our problems; instead we are treated to denial methods and ways to blunt the pain.

Too often we overlook the obvious. The cross of Christ and the promise of peace is extended to us as a free and unconditional gift. St. Paul is very clear on this point. He states: "We have peace with God through our Lord Jesus Christ." The peace Paul speaks of is more than an inner feeling. It is the very condition of our Christian life as given to us through Jesus Christ. It is our very relationship to God as was made known to us on the cross of Calvary. The first comfort of the cross is the promise of peace with God. We are no longer at odds with God, nor is he at odds with us. There is no obstacle between us and a loving heavenly Father who comforts us and receives us as his own children. As Jesus says in the Gospel of John, "Peace I leave with you; my peace I give to you; not as the world gives do I give to you" (John 14:27).

Much more can be said about the comfort of the cross. Having peace is one thing, but what about the separation of death as a time of trial and testing? It is a natural thing to question our own salvation and relationship to God at a time like this. God has given a life of joy and meaning with a beloved wife and mother, but now sorrow tries and tests us. Have we fallen from God's grace? Have we encountered a "no access" sign in our Christian lives? Perhaps we ask, "Has the gift of grace suddenly been taken from us?" St. Paul is again very clear at this point. Certainly we haven't fallen from God's grace. Just as the promise of peace is a comfort of the cross, so also the gift of grace is a comfort of the cross. It is a gift because we haven't earned God's attitude toward us, nor have we earned or merited Christ's saving work for us.

To have the gift of grace is always to have access to God's love, understanding, and forgiveness. It is to know with certainty that God will not shut us out. That, friends in Christ, is the second comfort we have today. It is the comfort of knowing and believing that the gift of grace is with us. As surely as Jesus of Nazareth lived, died, and was raised from the dead, so also we can be assured that God's grace, our access to him as sinners, has not been closed.

There is much more comfort in the cross of Christ. Even as we mourn today we are not without the thought that tomorrow will come. We will have to begin another day without a loving wife and mother. What will take her place? Who can take her place? Is there anything to look forward to? Is there any hope? Giving up is too easy. I don't think your wife and mother would have you become immersed in your sorrow and pity— she would have you live on to your fullest. You farmers know that many times you are the victims of nature; hot winds, minimal rainfall, and high temperatures wither the crops and leave the land dusty and unproductive. But, if you have hope, if you can look to the next year, you will be moved to plant again and look forward to a successful harvest.

Today we look to the future even though it is difficult because one whom we loved and who returned our love has been separated from us in death. Yet, as Christians we dare look to the future, to the next day, the next week and the next year because the hand of hope is extended to us through Jesus Christ. This third comfort of the cross, the hand of hope, is that which leads us to rejoice and be confident, not in ourselves but in God. The hand of hope is God reaching for us through his Son, Jesus Christ, so that we might be led into the future with him. Our future is solidly linked to God through Jesus Christ who leads us into his future glory. Grasp that hand of hope in Christ; he will enable you to face the future unafraid because he has promised to be with you.

I would have you remember that the cross of Christ is where we find comfort when we are in sorrow or distress. In the cross we find the promise of peace with God, the gift of grace which gives us access to him, and the hand of hope which leads us to greater glory with God. My prayer for you today as you stand in the shadow of the cross is that you may find peace with God, thrive in his grace and grasp the open hand of hope which leads to eternal life with God the Father. Amen.

THE PREACHER—Lowell O. Erdahl is a native of Blue Earth, Minnesota. He is a graduate of St. Olaf College, Northfield, Luther Theological Seminary, St. Paul, and Union Theological Seminary, New York City. His first parish was in Farmington, Minnesota, after which he served as instructor in homiletics at Luther Seminary. He is now pastor of University Lutheran Church of Hope, Minneapolis.

THE OCCASION—The sermon was preached at the funeral of a young wife and mother who committed suicide. She had been hospitalized frequently for severe depression and had talked about suicide on numerous occasions. Her mother had also been a suicide.

THE COMMENTS—The pastor does a masterful job with a difficult situation. He first deals with the problem posed by the act, then he speaks of guilt felt by the mourners and includes himself in that guilt. Finally he applies the comfort of the word of God. Not every suicide can be discussed so openly in a sermon but here it is done with sincerity and love.

The Final Healing

As we meet together this afternoon we share many
deep feelings . . .

    feelings of grief and guilt
    feelings of frustration and failure
    feelings of bereavement and bewilderment
    feelings of loss and loneliness.

Words are not enough to express everything we feel at
a time like this.

Beyond these feelings there are questions. We wonder "Why?" and there is none to answer.

Was it fear and weariness?

Was it even love and sacrifice acting in a way our
minds can't perceive?

Was it in search of one who had taken the same way
long years before?

We wonder why and there is none to answer.

We cannot know—God only knows.

Those of us who were privileged to have known Jean
and to have her tell us something of her deep fears
and feelings, have known for years that Jean suffered
—and suffered deeply—from an illness of mind and

emotion. Her picture of herself was so different from our picture of her.

To us so strong
so talented
so able
so much to give
so often giving.

We have memories now of how her life made our lives better for having known her.

But to herself, sometimes at least—in down moods and times of depression—there appeared a different picture:

Weak
a failure
a burden.

The difference between the way we saw Jean and the way she sometimes saw herself is, I think, the measure of the depth of her illness—the illness from which she died.

Having been privileged to have known something of Jean's inner life, I sincerely believe that Jean died of an illness—an illness as real as cancer—an illness for which she received the best medical treatment that was available. But the treatment, as is often the case with cancer, does not always cure.

Yet this recognition of Jean's illness does not remove all our feelings of guilt and failure. Some of these are false feelings. We have not failed at everything. We have too many good memories to believe that.

But some of these feelings are true—we have all failed—none of us is perfect, we have made mistakes—we have done what we shouldn't have done, we have said what we shouldn't have said, we have left undone and unsaid much we should have done and said. We have, every one of us, been far less than the person God meant us to be.

To talk this way is not to berate ourselves but only to be honest. No parishioner ever had a perfect pastor, and Jean didn't either. I feel a sense of having failed, and I am sure that these feelings reflect a measure of truth. Some of you also have similar feelings. None of us ever had a perfect father or mother, a perfect husband or a perfect wife, none of us is a perfect person. We feel our imperfections today, and so we confess our failures. Yet in making our confession we do not condemn ourselves for God does not condemn us. We know that our failures are real, but we know they are not too big for God to forgive. Whatever our feelings may be, no matter how guilty we are or feel, we are not condemned, we are loved. As we face our real failures, we do so in the presence of God's real grace. We can then once again learn what forgiveness really means.

Forgiveness from God who really loves and cares—

Forgiveness from God who loves us now in all our fears and our failings, in all of our doubts and distress—

Forgiveness from God, who in his mercy accepts us and loves us as we are.

And so we turn from ourselves, away from our feelings, and turn toward the presence and promises of God. To turn our thoughts in this direction we consider two passages in the New Testament. Both of these are passages Jean had marked in her Bible. As have so many in our congregation, Jean had purchased a copy of the new translation, *Today's English Version*. She told me just a week or so ago that she had read a good deal in this New Testament and she had marked two passages in it. One of these passages includes these verses from the eighth chapter of Paul's letter to the Romans. I begin reading with verse thirty-five:

> Who, then, can separate us from the love of Christ? Can trouble do it, or hardship or persecution or hunger or poverty or danger or death? . . . No, in all these things we have complete victory through him who loved us! For I am certain that nothing can separate us from his love: neither death nor life, neither angels nor other heavenly rulers or powers, neither present nor the future, neither the world above nor the world below— there is nothing in all creation that will ever be able to separate us from the love of God which is ours through Christ Jesus our Lord.

Think of that promise—nothing in life or in death, nothing in all creation can separate us from the love of God, in Christ Jesus our Lord. As Jean marked this passage in her New Testament and in her mind, so also today, we mark this passage in our minds, and brand it upon our hearts.

Nothing—Nothing—*Nothing*—can separate us from the love of God, which is in Christ Jesus, our Lord. Nothing that we can do, nothing that anyone can do, nothing can ever stop God from loving us. To that great love, that love that loves each of us more than we can love ourselves, love that none can ever stop, to that love we entrust Jean, and to that love we also entrust ourselves. In confident trust of his mercy, and with de-

pendence upon his care, we give ourselves to that great
and gracious love of God.

The other passage that Jean had marked was from
the Gospel of Mark, including the last paragraphs of
the fifth chapter. These paragraphs tell of two events. I
will not read them but simply recount the story for you.
The first is the story of the woman who had been ill
for twelve years. It says she had sought help from
many doctors, and that she found no healing until she
touched the hem of Jesus' garment. Then she was
healed. The last paragraph of this chapter tells of Jesus
restoring life to Jairus' daughter. When this happened,
the account says those who witnessed it "were com-
pletely amazed" (Mark 5:42 TEV).

Jean also sought healing in this world. For about
twelve years, she, too, went for help to many doctors.
In this world there are some illnesses that are not
healed, but this world does not have the last word.
The failure of the earth's physicians is not a final failure, for beyond the physicians of this world is a Great
Physician. In his love and power, he promises healing,
total and final healing, in resurrection and life eternal.
To the loving and healing power of the Great and Good
Physician we entrust one we loved. To that same Physician we also entrust our own lives, depending upon his
love every moment, living in confident trust and certain
hope of the final healing, of resurrection and life
eternal.

THE PREACHER—Hoover T. Grimsby was born in Viroqua, Wisconsin. He was educated at the University of Minnesota and at Luther Theological Seminary. He has served as pastor at Ascension Church, Milwaukee, St. Olaf's in Austin, Minnesota and is presently serving at Central Lutheran Church in Minneapolis.

THE OCCASION — The sermon was preached for the death of an aged member of the church.

THE COMMENTS—The language used by the preacher is very fine. The sermon is outstanding in the use of illustrative material. The stories come from many areas and hold our attention but they also help to develop the message.

From the
Point of No Return

One of the remarkable stories in American history is told in connection with the Trappist Monastery of Gethsemani in Kentucky. It is said that one member of the first body of monks to come to Gethsemani from France in 1848 had been a soldier under Napoleon and was at Boulogne in 1804 when the invasion of Britain was noisily preparing. British ships of war were guarding the harbor of Boulogne in blockade force. One day when a storm blew off the coast, Napoleon called for volunteers to swim out, cut the cables of the British ships, and let them be swept away by the storm. Of the volunteers only one succeeded in cutting a cable under musket fire from the ship. He made his way back to shore with a bullet in his shoulder. Napoleon met him on the beach, took the cross of the legion of honor from his own tunic and placed it in the hands of this soldier.

This soldier, after Waterloo, came to Gethsemani in 1848 and from then on was sealed in silence and seclusion. When at last the monk came to die on the ash-strewn floor, the abbot, as usual, gave him the final dispensation from silence, saying, "If you have anything to say, you may speak in peace." And the veteran of Napoleon and of God, turned his head feebly and asked, "What became of the emperor?"

On Good Friday afternoon, nineteen centuries ago, a few choice souls saw Jesus of Nazareth, whom they had accepted and hailed as the Christ, die upon the cross. At this sight the chosen twelve were driven to despair and were ready to go back to their old occupations. Peter declared, "I'm going fishing," and the others said, "We will go with you." All of them feared for their lives and hid themselves from their enemies. All their hopes had been dashed to pieces. Christ's kingdom seemed a horrible nightmare. They thought his cause was defeated and lost. When Rome crucified a man he was dead. As far as the disciples were concerned, that was the end of Jesus. They never even bothered to ask the question, "What became of the Master?"

As we stood beneath the cross of Jesus last Good Friday afternoon, the same feeling of the disciples crept over us. Death is strictly the end of our earthly existence. Through death all our relationships of love and friendship are severed. For us death is a complete loss, it is as far as our earthly existence is concerned, final. From death there is no return.

Some time ago I read an article written by the president of a large commercial airline. In this article he was speaking about the huge airships that are flying back and forth across our seven seas daily. Of special interest to me was his description of the instrument panel on each of these great airships. There is one instrument which charts the entire course, telling how many miles have been flown, and how many are left to fly. On this instrument is an arrow that keeps moving toward a red line. That red line is called "the point of no return." It is called that because when the plane has gone that far, the fuel supplies are used up to such an extent that the ship cannot go back to the base.

That phrase, "The point of no return" caught my attention because it seemed so typical of the idea which so many people had at the time of Jesus concerning his grave. In spite of the prophecy of the Old Testament, in spite of Christ's words themselves, these people looked at his grave as a point of no return. For them there was no possibility of a resurrection. But Christ arose from the dead and said, "Because I live, you shall live also."

As we hear the answer to the question uppermost in our minds, "What became of the Master?" we do not close our eyes, turn our head and make no other sign as did the veteran of Napoleon. No indeed, for we have no dead hope but a living hope by the resurrection of Jesus Christ from the dead. Our problem is that living in the shadows, our eyes have not as yet accommodated themselves to the dazzling splendor of the life that has been brought to the light by the gospel of the Easter resurrection of our Lord.

Speaking of good news, where will you find better news than the angel's declaration: "He is not here, for he has risen, as he said." The good news we share with one another today is the Gospel. That is always good news, even though the wages of sin bring only death. Faith, which itself is a gift from God, opens new vistas as it attaches itself to the Easter truth which dispels the darkness and mystery from the future. Death is not the last word about ourselves and our destiny, and that of our loved ones. God who has given us life has set eternity into our hearts, and our hearts are restless until they rest in him. His triumphant action in raising Jesus from the dead is our assurance for the future.

In the 16th century during the reigns of Charles V and Philip II, Spain stamped the pillars of Hercules guarding the Mediterranean on her own coins, underneath was struck the inscription, *Ne Plus Ultra*—nothing beyond. Then the sailor, Columbus, pointed his little fleet of boats toward the sunset, and having left the long leagues of blue sea behind him, found a new world. Spain by necessity revised her motto to read *Plus Ultra*—more beyond.

When Christ set sail over the seas of life, past the point of no return, and came back with the charts of eternity, people cried out *Plus Ultra*—there is more beyond. Jesus himself is our assurance that faith in life in him is eternal. "If it were not so, I would have told you." Our faith rests on his reliability. He would not deceive us.

A little boy was sitting on an ocean pier—one of the many that line the Pacific Coast in Oregon. As he was sitting there dangling his feet over the end of the pier his thinking was rudely interrupted by a stranger. The stranger said, "What do you suppose lies out there in the distant west, far beyond the roll of the waves?" In the twinkling of an eye came the answer: "The Orient, of course." Much astonished at the little fellow's knowledge, the man inquired, "How do you know?" and the little fellow again quickly replied, saying, "My dad's a sailor, and he has been over there, and has come back here and told me so."

We too have one who has been over there and has come back here and told us so, the Lord Jesus Christ. He came back from the point of no return, and gave us the blessed assurance that life and faith in him never end, but are constantly being made new, here and hereafter. He says, "Let not your heart be troubled. In my Father's house are many mansions." He is our authority for believing that our loved one in Christ, we shall see again. "I am the resurrection and the life, he that believes in me though he were dead, yet shall he live." To prove it all, he died and rose again, and became the first fruits of them that sleep. He encourages us saying, "Be of good cheer, I have overcome the world."

This is good news which is really good. With Peter we can cry out, "Blessed be the God and Father of our Lord Jesus Christ, who in his abundant mercy has brought us again to a living hope by the resurrection of Jesus Christ from the dead."

THE PREACHER—John Victor Halvorson was born in New London, Minnesota. He is a graduate of Luther College, Luther Seminary, the University of Minnesota, Johns Hopkins University and Union Seminary, Richmond, Virginia. Besides being on the faculty at Luther Seminary in St. Paul, Minnesota for a number of years, he has served parishes in Washington, Minnesota and South Dakota. He is currently pastor of Bethlehem Lutheran Church, Aberdeen, South Dakota.

THE OCCASION — The sermon was preached as a memorial sermon for a man past middle age who had died a peaceable death.

THE COMMENTS—The material in the sermon is theological but fitting under the circumstances. There is a good blending of personal and biblical material here. The Niebuhr quotation toward the end is thought-provoking and might form the basis of a good funeral meditation.

The Christian Hope

Martha said to Jesus, "Lord, if you had been here, my brother would not have died. And even now I know that whatever you ask from God, God will give you." Jesus said to her, "Your brother will rise again." Martha said to him, "I know that he will rise again in the resurrection at the last day." Jesus said to her, "I am the resurrection and the life; he who believes in me, though he die, yet shall he live, and whoever believes in me shall never die. Do you believe this?" She said to him, "Yes, Lord; I believe that you are the Christ, the Son of God, he who is coming into the world."   John 11:21-27

These past years Dr. Frank Schultz has been in the hospital from time to time. This has provided me an opportunity to visit with him on a number of occasions. I must admit that my visits with Dr. Schultz have been some of the most intriguing which I have had as a pastor. He would tell me about his German immigrant parents and how they worked to make it at the time when he was born in 1901. He also loved to tell about his struggle to obtain his education. This culminated when he received his Ph.D. from the University of Minnesota in 1941.

One thing was always evident. Frank was a true

67

scholar. He had a love of learning and wisdom. When he went to the hospital Frank would have some books with him. As we visited I would ask, "What are you reading?" Frequently one or more of those books would be in the area of philosophy. One aspect which interested him was existentialism.

I want to share this incident with you because it discloses something about Frank, who was a gifted teacher. I would say to him, "Frank, how do you understand existentialism?" This was his reply to me: "In order to understand existentialism you have to see it in relationship to two other positions in the history of thought. The one is idealism. Idealism has its own view of truth. Idealism tries to get God's perspective on things. This is its view of truth. The other position is naturalism and here truth is a matter of correspondence. It is the correspondence between the object out there and yourself as the knowing subject." Then he would come to existentialism. Frank would say, "This is something different. Here truth is a quality of human life. Your life and my life is a kind of truth."

About this time I would speak up and say, "Frank, you remember that in the Gospel of John, Jesus once said, 'I am the truth.'" At that, Frank would nod his head for he was a deeply religious man. This did not mean that he suspended his powers of reflection. Frank loved to ask questions about the mysteries of faith. One area which intrigued him was the area of Christian hope.

It is fitting then that we look at a biblical story about hope today. I have chosen the familiar episode from the Gospel of John, the story of the death of Lazarus that leads up to Jesus' great claim: "I am the resurrection and the life. He that believes in me, though he were dead, yet shall he live. He that believes in me shall live today." Martha then replies to these great words with her confession of faith.

What does this incident in the life of our Lord say to us today? Lazarus had passed away. Death had come to him. Does physical death point to something? It is a sign. It points to the biblical and human understanding of man. God created man from the dust. This is the Bible's way of saying that I am a creature. God also created Adam in his image and told him: "Have dominion over the earth and subdue it.

In other words, the image of God means the creative freedom which God gave to man. This means that you and I are creatures and creators. In the Garden of Eden Adam lived in a relationship of responsibility and trust to God. Then came Adam's desire to be the pure creator and to be like God. This led to rebellion and it was in that rebellion that death, as we know it, entered this world. Death then is a sign and a symbol. It is a reminder to me that I have rebelled and sinned. This is why death comes with sudden shock. It is a separation from each other, but the question confronts us: "Is it also a separation from God?"

The New Testament is very emphatic that God has acted to restore us. Something has entered this world already in the person of Jesus Christ. Something new has come. But on the cross Christ died. It looked as if this would end everything. Then came Easter. He rose and is alive. In his death Christ took our rebellion upon himself. In Christ God acted to make restoration possible. Death need not be a separation from God. The New Testament says that when death comes we are at home with the Lord. The Apostle Paul contends that Christ's resurrection is the first fruits of our resurrection.

Now, is this Christian hope practical for us? Is it an escape from responsibility in this world? A remarkable leader among our churches in America was Reinhold Niebuhr. As a young pastor he had a very liberal education. Then he came to his first parish in Detroit in 1915. He has written about this in a book called *Beyond Tragedy.* He admits that he did not take seriously the confession, "I believe in the Resurrection of the body." Then he tells us, "After a few years I began to see this as one of the most basic elements in the Christian faith. It affirms that God wants our whole self to be with Him forever." "Furthermore," Niebuhr points out, "the way we understand our ultimate end determines how we understand ourselves now as believers. If my whole self is to be with God forever in Heaven, this means that my whole self is involved with God right now."

The Christian faith did two things for Dr. Frank Schultz. It attached him to this world. Frank loved life. He loved his work and he loved his family. One did not visit with him for long before he sensed Frank's great interest in his students. But the Christian faith also *detached* Frank from this world. He knew he was a citizen of another kingdom. He could say with the Apostle Paul in Romans 14:8, "If we live, we live with the Lord; if we die, we die with the Lord. So then, whether we live or whether we die we are the Lord's."

God bless his memory among us.

THE PREACHER—Larry A. Hoffsis is a native of Crawford County, Ohio. He is a graduate of Capital University and Lutheran Theological Seminary, both in Columbus, Ohio, and of Heidelberg University in Germany. He began his ministry at Sidney, Ohio, and at present is pastor of Trinity Lutheran Church in Columbus.

THE OCCASION—Patsy S. was born with a rare blood disease. She spent a great deal of time in the hospital but also did well in her studies and was able to complete her confirmation instruction. She died at the age of sixteen.

THE COMMENTS—The sermon radiates warm pastoral concern. The preacher uses personal illustrations effectively. This type of material can backfire, but in this sermon each illustration is appropriate. The careful outline and textual development is exemplary.

With the Good Shepherd

He shall feed his flock like a shepherd: he shall gather
the lambs with his arm, and carry them in his bosom.
Isaiah 40:11 (KJV)

Remember the green hymnal? The one we used for
Sunday school openings when Patsy was in grade
school? Everyone who attended our Sunday school became familiar with the opening service on page 5. I
have learned that children, including Patsy, loved one
phase in that opening dialog. It began with the leader
of the assembly saying, "He shall feed his flock like a
shepherd." Then everyone would respond: "He shall
gather the lambs with his arm and carry them in his
bosom."

Patsy and I spoke those phrases once again just a few
days ago in the hospital. Both of us agreed they were
great phrases. You will do well if in your grief you can
speak quietly these same words, "He shall feed his
flock like a shepherd." Then listen for her confident
response: "He has gathered me with his arm and carries me in his bosom." In this way you will be comforted in knowing she is with the Good Shepherd.

These words also form the text of one of the most

beautiful solos in George Frederick Handel's great work, *The Messiah*. The title of that work should point us to the fulfillment of the promises of God stated by Isaiah, namely, that the Shepherd who feeds his flock, and gathers the lambs in his arm and carries them in his bosom is none other than Jesus. Did he not say, "I am the Good Shepherd, I know my own, my own know me!"

Be assured about Patsy. She is with the Good Shepherd! The Good Shepherd is Jesus!

It will be helpful for us, though, to spend a few moments exploring the depths of meaning contained in these phrases which Patsy knew by heart and trusted.

1. How can we know for sure that the Good Shepherd's flock included Patsy? How could she know for sure? After all, a physical condition like hers could make one feel rejected by God. For that assurance we must remember her Baptism. I have always thought that Baptism is not for God's assurance; it is for ours.

I want to illustrate that statement with a reference to my own father. My father always kept sheep. Each spring our farm would almost be overrun with ewes and lambs. Soon after each lamb was born, father would put his identifying mark on its back. The marking of these new lambs was not for my father's benefit but for our neighbors. He was always able to identify his own even without seeing the red "H" on its back. Similarly Jesus said, "I know my own, and my own know me."

Baptism has many deep meanings. Perhaps the most important meaning that Baptism can have for us right now is to assure us, as Patsy was assured, that she was indeed a lamb in the flock of the Good Shepherd. Whether she was at home, in a hospital room or almost hidden away in the intensive care unit, she knew, as we should know, that she belonged to God's flock. That's why I can say to you, be assured about Patsy. She is with the Good Shepherd!

2. We should also take comfort in the phrase, "He shall feed his flock." In the Lord's Prayer we pray that God would give us daily bread. Indeed he does. He used you, father, to work for it for your family; you, mother, to prepare it. But I also know your frustrations with daily bread. There came a time in which Patsy couldn't take nourishment from daily bread in its usual forms. Feeding had to be done intravenously. But even that was not enough. The Good Shepherd never intended that it would be the only kind of feeding he could do.

An old hymn asks of Jesus that he would break the bread of life for us just as surely as he broke "the loaves beside the sea." This hymn looks at Scripture and the words of Jesus as being an even more significant "bread" to sustain life—not just for a lifetime but for eternity.

As we know, Jesus does spread a table. He feeds us with more than his words. He gives himself to us. How wonderful—beyond the food on the hospital tray, beyond the intravenous feeding, the Good Shepherd provided a way to feed all his children. "Take and eat, this is my body, given for you. Take and drink, this is my blood, shed for you."

3. I have a special image in mind when I hear the words "gathers the lambs with his arm." One of my

early memories is of my father taking me, as a small boy, to a pasture we had rented to provide additional grazing for our flock.

As we walked to the far side of this property, we came to a small stream of water which we needed to cross. When it became apparent that my fear was too great to attempt leaping it, my father simply reached down, took me in his strong right arm and leaped to the other side.

In walking with the Good Shepherd, Patsy came to the edge of this life. The other side was not frightening to her. It was the chasm between two lives that seemed so formidable.

We didn't talk as freely about the chasm and the other side as I think now we might have done. But we were both sure about what would happen. The Shepherd would gather her in his arm and carry her through death to everlasting life.

Moses wrote, "The eternal God is your dwelling place, and underneath are the everlasting arms." Once when young children were brought to Jesus, his disciples, meaning to be helpful, tried to keep them at arm's length. But Jesus said, "Let the children come to be, do not hinder them, for to such belongs the kingdom of God." And he took them up in his arms and blessed them, laying his hands upon them. It is the Good Shepherd's practice, to gather the lambs with his arms.

"O sing to the Lord a new song," counseled one of the psalmists, "for he has done marvelous things. His right hand and his holy arm have gotten him the victory." We know the Lord's great victory. It is the victory over sin and death which Jesus has won for us. His hands nailed to the cross, his holy arms suspended from the crossbar—this has gotten him the victory. The marvelous thing is—it was for Patsy. It's for us all.

4. Finally, consider the meaning of the last phrase, "carry them in his bosom." We have many fanciful pictures of eternal life. I hope we are not misled by them. Rather than making our children into angels in heaven, or seeing them walk through gates of pearl and down streets of gold, let us be content with the image of this Scripture which Patsy knew so well.

I know of no scene of greater safety and peace than that of a child at mother's bosom. It is the epitome of tenderness and closeness.

A way of thinking of heaven is to picture it as being in the bosom of the heavenly Father. In the bosom of the Father there is safety and peace, tenderness and closeness far beyond our hopes and dreams.

When St. John was describing the relationship of Jesus to the Father in heaven, he used the same image. "No one has ever seen God, the only Son who is in the bosom of the Father, he has made him known."

What comfort it is to know that these words were on Patsy's lips and in her heart as this life ebbed out and the same strong arms that carried the cross could gather her and carry her in his bosom.

I have seen how lovingly you carried her—to the hospital, back home, back to the hospital again. She was next to you, close to you, often in your arms. But you could not carry her through death. And now you have given her over to the strong arms of the Good Shepherd.

THE PREACHER—Reginald H. Holle was born in Burton, Texas. He is a graduate of Texas Lutheran College, Seguin, Texas, Capital University and Lutheran Theological Seminary, both of Columbus, Ohio, and Wittenberg University, Springfield, Ohio. He has served as pastor of Zion Church, Sandusky, Ohio, of Salem Memorial in Detroit, and of Parma Lutheran Church, Cleveland. He is at present Bishop of the Michigan District of The American Lutheran Church.

THE OCCASION—The sermon was preached for the death of a church member who suffered a cerebral hemorrhage at the age of 70. He had been a gardener and a greenhouse owner.

THE COMMENTS—The occupation of an individual often affords the starting point for a funeral. In this sermon the pastor uses the concept of a garden not only as a starting point but as the basic structure for the entire sermon. Such an effort is one that will be well remembered by the mourners.

In the Garden

The Lord will guide you continually, and satisfy your desire with good things, and make your bones strong, and you shall be like a watered garden, like a spring of water, whose waters fail not.   Isaiah 58:11

The fruitful gardens at the Christensen Greenhouse are symbolic of Carl's life and faith. His skills with soil, with seed, light, and water have sent produce to the market, plants to homes, Easter lilies and Christmas poinsettias to churches for almost fifty years. His deep faith in the Lord who brings growth and harvest sustained the master gardener in changing seasons.

Those memories have bolstered us in the uncertain hours in the emergency and intensive care rooms. They encouraged us to grasp the hand of the Good Shepherd as it became obvious that he was leading us through the dark valley of the shadow of death. Now it is possible to raise our voices in a chorus of praise to the "Beautiful Savior, King of Creation . . . (who) makes our sorrowing spirit sing." We offer our petitions to the Creator who promises growth where seed is planted *in the garden.*

On Sunday, Clark and his wife were in these pews

79

and participated in the sacrament of Holy Communion in their faithful pattern of devotion and commitment to Christ and his family. The promise of Isaiah was fulfilled in our sacramental sharing: "You shall be like a watered garden, like a spring of water, whose waters fail not." The cleansing, refreshing and nourishing gifts of Holy Communion provide the springs of living water, even in the face of death's dark clouds.

God's family is invited to come into the garden. Where seeds are buried in the ground with adequate water and light, there is a promise of growth and fruit. As we lay the body of the gardener into the ground, we trust the creator's promise and await the fruits of our Christian faith. "The Lord will guide you continually and satisfy your desire with good things . . . and you shall be like a watered garden."

"The Lord God planted a garden in Eden" (Gen. 2:8). In the introductory chapters of Scripture, the Father sets the human family in the garden. There are trees pleasant to the sight and good for food and the river flows to water the garden. Man is put into that garden to till it and keep it. You know that the only restriction in the idyllic setting is the tree of the knowledge of good and evil, a reminder that God sets boundaries for the fruitful life.

Carl would have been thrilled to be the gardener in Eden. His careful cultivation of plants in the greenhouse demonstrated a respect for the Father's creation. His awareness of the potential in the tiniest seed expressed his faith in God who gives the increase.

Last spring Mr. Christiansen held a thimbleful of petunia seeds in his hands and provided me with an object lesson regarding the thousands of plants, blossoms and brightness contained there. He was eager to have the greenhouse filled with trees that are pleasant to sight and plants good for food. Flowers, houseplants, tomatoes, endive and a host of other growing things re-created a bit of Eden on Schaaf Road that has been scattered around the community and nation.

The Creator shares Eden's opportunities with us also. He offers to provide the resources that can make life beautiful and worthwhile. He assigns the responsibility for providing food for our families and the expanded world family to his people. As you and I live in the garden of plenty, there is the constant temptation to resist the Creator's command to share our blessings. The "tree of the knowledge of good and evil" lures us into schemes that would ignore the needs of others as we focus on ourselves.

Then there is the call of the Garden of Gethsemane where Jesus invites us to join him in watchfulness and prayer. Recall the sorrowful and troubled Christ who prayed: "My Father, if it be possible, let this cup pass from me; nevertheless, not as I will, but as thou wilt" (Matt. 26:39).

That petition resounded in the cubicle of the emergency room on Sunday evening. Troubled and sorrowful, we prayed together confident that the Father's will would be done. Our hope was that the cup containing death's potion would be removed; but as believers at Gethsemane's garden, we submitted to the Father's will. Christ is here and he takes us into the Father's presence and power.

Gethsemane calls for realism in our faith. The way

of the cross leads us into suffering and pain, and death itself. Jesus calls us to take up the cross and follow him. Yet the way of glory appeals to us and urges us to ignore the place of prayer and struggle. Carl understood this garden and lived in its struggles in the midst of life. He was strong in his faith and confident in the Christ as crises came to the family and to his business. In the agony of Donna's tumor (his granddaughter) our brother prayed more earnestly "and his sweat became like great drops of blood falling down upon the earth."

Even though the effects of that Gethsemane continue to hover over you, the faith of your husband, father and grandfather will be an inspiration through the years. Encouragement, strength, joy, and hope stemming from a strong faith have not been limited to your family. Our parish community has been blessed by the visits you have made on fellow-members in their loneliness, illness, and need. Your unselfish dedication of time and skill to the various groups of the church has enriched all of us. Your Danish friends resound with praise for your cheerful and strong presence in both the Gardens of Eden and Gethsemane, their hours of celebration and pain.

Now we walk into the Garden of Victory promised by the Living Christ. Our Lord who has conquered death's sting and robbed the grave of victory offers his assuring note: "Blessed are those who wash their robes, that they may have the right to the tree of life and that they may enter the city by the gates" (Rev. 22:14).

When we have been washed and made white in the blood of the Lamb, then you and I gain the victory over death. Then we share in the joys and blessings of the garden in glory that God gives his people by grace. Here is the sure and certain gift that places us in the everlasting garden of the Father. The present reality in Christ wipes away tears and provides strength and courage for the days ahead.

You and I have seen Jesus through our tears. The ominous clouds of death were evident during the five days that we waited and prayed. "Why are you weeping?" was the Master's query as we ministered to one another. Remember that Mary Magdalene could only see the gardener through her clouded eyes on Easter morning. But the Risen Lord was there and she could run to proclaim: "I have seen the Lord."

We too have seen the Risen Lord in the gardens with our gardener. "The Lord will guide you continually . . . and you shall be like a watered garden."

THE PREACHER—Bonnie Jensen is a native of Hartley, Iowa. She graduated from Dana College and at present is a student at Wartburg Seminary, Dubuque, Iowa, where her husband is a member of the faculty.

THE OCCASION—The sermon was originally prepared to fulfill a classroom assignment. It was later preached on the occasion of the death of an elderly member of a Dubuque church.

THE COMMENTS—The sermon is an excellent example of the preaching possibilities that are to be found in newer translations of the Bible. Good News for Modern Man provides the spark for the preacher's approach. Exploring new translations can be very rewarding. The sermon is also striking in that it presents the gospel in starkness and clarity, inviting the congregation to find complete comfort there.

Mortal and Immortal

Through the living and eternal word of God you have been born again as children of a parent who is immortal. As the scripture says, "All mankind are like grass, and their glory is like wild flowers. The grass withers, and the flowers fall, but the word of the Lord remains forever." This word is the Good News that was proclaimed to you.

1 Peter 1:23-25 (TEV)

It's never easy on days like this when we have to sit in the presence of a coffin, in the presence of the lifeless body of a dear one, in the presence of death itself. Our hearts are very heavy and our minds keep wishing there was some way of escape.

Sarah's life has ended. She lived a long life, a rich and full life. But now it's over. Sarah is gone from us, and we will miss her very much. Now her life is only a memory. The sound of her laugh, the flash of her eyes, the work of her hands—all is finished. It's done. Over.

As a child of mortal parents she has become the victim of her inherited mortality. From the day she was born, it has been true and evident that this day would come, when family and friends would have to gather together to return her to the earth. Because she was born of mortal parents, she has withered like the grass withers at the close of a season and the flower's petals fall to the ground. After a long life she has completed the cycle. She has died.

Today we are also aware that Sarah is not the only child of mortal parents. We all are. And the illness or death of someone we know such as Sarah reminds us of that. I too am a child of mortal parents. You too are the child of mortal parents. That's one thing about being human that we cannot escape. We are born to die. As the Preacher in Ecclesiastes puts it: "Vanity of vanities! All is vanity." Emptiness, emptiness. All is empty. "What does man gain by all the toil at which he toils under the sun? A generation goes and a generation comes, but the earth remains forever." And a little further on he writes: "For the fate of the sons of men and the fate of beasts is the same; as one dies, so dies the other. Death comes to both alike."

Because we are born of mortal parents, we are all victims of mortality. The end comes for all of us.

As Christians, however, we know that's not the last word to be spoken over our lives. Our text reminds us that we are also born of a parent who is immortal. We have experienced a second birth. "Our Father, who art in heaven," we say. *Our Father.* We are children of a heavenly Father.

Time and again through these past eighty years Sarah said those familiar words, "Our Father." She was the child of an immortal, everlasting parent. And children of an immortal, everlasting parent inherit immortality.

This second childhood, this second birth was a birth

by the power of the word of God—nothing else. Sarah heard this word often. Jesus forgives you, Sarah. Jesus loves you. Jesus gives you new birth.

Jesus gives us immortality. We are born again into an eternal family. Each time Sarah heard that word, and each time we hear that word we are born again in immortality.

There are many signs here today that remind us of Sarah's mortality. Almost everything that we see—coffin, tears, sorrow, even the flowers soon to wither—remind us that Sarah was a mortal. Death, the inheritance from her human parents, is very vivid, very much with us at this moment.

Only one thing stands over against this death, only one thing—the Word of God. "The grass withers, the flower falls, but the word of the Lord remains forever." And that word is the good news which was preached to you, the good news of Jesus Christ, crucified and alive again, for Sarah's sake and for ours, the good news that Jesus Christ brings a new birth, a new parent and a new inheritance of immortality. That's all we have when death knocks. That's all we have on the day of a funeral. That's all we have when the grass dies and its flowers fall—the Word, which is the good news of Jesus Christ.

All that is left for Sarah today is this Word. She has been stripped of everything else. Nothing else remains, no breath, no consciousness, no heartbeat, not even a confession of faith on her lips. Life is gone. All there is for Sarah today is the Word, which is the good news of Jesus Christ, preached to her many times over the years and preached to us today.

When our day of death comes, when we are stripped of our health and our life and our breath, only one thing will remain, only hope will remain. And that hope is that God will keep his word, that Jesus will indeed come again to raise us up, that we are indeed children of an immortal parent, Our Father who art in heaven. That is all. But that is enough.

THE PREACHER—Michael W. Kerr was born in Dayton, Ohio. He is a graduate of Pacific Lutheran University. At the time he wrote this sermon, Michael was a student at Wartburg Seminary in Dubuque, Iowa.

THE OCCASION—The sermon was prepared to fulfill a classroom requirement in homiletics at the seminary. The preacher wrote it for the funeral of a woman who died following a brief illness.

THE COMMENTS—The season of the church year can be an effective starting point for a funeral sermon. The preacher here uses the time of death as a motif for the entire sermon. The theology of "the wounded God" may seem deep for a funeral and yet the message presented here is clear and easily grasped.

A Time of Dyings

And his father Zechariah was filled with the Holy Spirit, and prophesied, saying, "Blessed be the Lord God of Israel, for he has visited and redeemed his people, and has raised up a horn of salvation for us in the house of his servant David, as he spoke by the mouth of his holy prophets from of old, that we should be saved from our enemies and from the hand of all who hate us; to perform the mercy promised to our fathers, and to remember his holy covenant, the oath which he swore to our father Abraham, to grant us that we, being delivered from the hand of our enemies, might serve him without fear, in holiness and righteousness before him all the days of our life. And you, child, will be called the prophet of the Most High; for you will go before the Lord to prepare his ways, to give knowledge of salvation to his people in the forgiveness of their sins, through the tender mercy of our God, when the day shall dawn upon us from on high to give light to those who sit in darkness and in the shadow of death, to guide our feet into the way of peace."

Luke 1:67-79

It is winter again. The snow lies heavily on the ground; the trees are barren; the skies are often gray. We are in a time of dyings, this winter season, when the earth herself seems to have surrendered her life to

snow and ice and chill winds, surrounding us with a
dark silence. And now we are plunged even more deeply into winter because Carol, known to us in so many
different ways—friend, mother, wife—has died along
with the earth, leaving only our memories of her to fill
the emptiness. Here is the hardest reality and the most
final thing we know in this life, the great enemy that
stills the sounds of life and imposes a silence around us
like the silence of winter.

Yet it is in the very midst of this time of dyings, this
winter season, that we Christians have long chosen to
begin our Church Year, even as the calendar year and
the life of the earth draw to a close. This is the season of Advent, four weeks of preparation and expec-
tation before the festival of Christmas. And one of the
Bible texts we ponder during Advent is the Song of
Zechariah, which I read a moment ago.

But what has such a hymn of praise about God coming to his people to do with us gathered in this place
in what seems more the absence than the presence of
God? Carol and we who mourn her have not been delivered out of the hand of our enemy death at all, but
rather have been overtaken by its power. Where, then,
is this visitation and redemption of God, this horn of
salvation raised up for us? Where is God now for Carol
and for us?

The answer, if indeed there can be any, is in what
Zechariah's song is really about. St. Luke places this
passage right before his story about Jesus' birth so that
Zechariah anticipates the coming, the Advent of Jesus
the Christ. Zechariah, as it were, introduces the whole
familiar wonder of the Christmas event, the manger in

Bethlehem, the choir of angels, the visiting shepherds, the beginnings of Jesus' life. But more than this, Zechariah anticipates the ending of Jesus' life, the stony hill outside Jerusalem, the mocking crowds, the nails and the cross. For this is where God has visited and redeemed us, in this Jesus crucified; this is how God has delivered us from the hand of our enemies, by Christ hanging on his cross, handed over to the power of death.

This is the mystery that Zechariah sings, that our God is a wounded God, one who knows the sorrow and grief of death, who knows from firsthand experience what it is to die and to have a loved one die. This God whom we call "Father" sent his own Son to be born of a woman like each of us, to laugh and weep with us, to talk and eat with us, and finally to die as each of us must die. This, I believe, is what Zechariah means when he says, "The day shall dawn upon us from on high to give light to those who sit in darkness and in the shadow of death." He means that God is with us here, in the face of Carol's death, in the cross of his Son Jesus, mourning with us, bidding us to share our sorrow with him. Our God is a wounded God, and we are a wounded people. We belong together.

But what about Carol's death, about death itself? Is not this enemy still with us, still to be defeated? It may seem so, but it isn't true. This Jesus whose coming Zechariah expected in his song and whose ending was crucifixion, this Jesus we believe God raised again in the resurrection as a promise to us that the last word in this life belongs not to death but to God. Just as Zechariah, before Jesus had even been born, sang his song as though God had already come to establish his reign, so we proclaim that victory belongs to God right here and now in the midst of Carol's death. Just as the day dawned on us from on high when Jesus was born, born to die, so by the faith God gives us in his Spirit, we hope and wait for the day when Jesus will come again to destroy that defeated enemy, death, a day when the dead will be raised and God's kingdom established in fullness of life.

It is winter again, a time of dyings. Yet we are alive in the midst of it, and our God who knows death, is alive in the midst of it with us. In the still darkness of the winter of Carol's death, Zechariah sings his Advent song about our wounded God. In her life Carol raised her voice in praise to this same crucified and risen Lord, and shared our Advent hope. Now, even in death she waits as we wait. So we say in the words of a familiar Advent hymn:

> O come thou Dayspring, come and cheer
> Our spirits by thine advent here;
> Disperse the gloomy clouds of night,
> And death's dark shadows put to flight.
> Rejoice, rejoice! Emmanuel
> Shall come to thee, O Israel.

THE PREACHER—Robert E. McClelland is a native of Memphis, Tennessee. He is a graduate of Southwestern College in Memphis, and of Wartburg Seminary, Dubuque, Iowa. He has served at Midvale Community Church, Madison, Wisconsin, at St. Peter's in Fennimore, Wisconsin, and at present is pastor of St. John Lutheran Church, Grafton, Wisconsin.

THE OCCASION—The sermon was preached for the death of a 70-year-old man who had been a faithful church member. He died suddenly.

THE COMMENTS—The sermon contains more personal material and eulogy than some of the others and yet the presentation is made carefully so that the glory goes to God. The hypothetical example early in the sermon is meaningful.

Finishing in Faith

For I am already on the point of being sacrificed; the time of my departure has come. I have fought the good fight, I have finished the race, I have kept the faith. Henceforth there is laid up for me the crown of righteousness, which the Lord, the righteous judge, will award to me on that Day, and not only to me but also to all who have loved his appearing.   2 Timothy 4:6-8

Death comes to everyone, yet no one fully understands what has happened. We know that at one moment someone is conscious in our presence, he is standing nearby, perhaps carrying on a conversation. He is able to move and think and act. And in another moment something happens to that body, and there is no more consciousness, there is no more response, there is no more breath. And the feeble way we describe this strange event is to say that life is gone—death has come.

There are various ways for a physician to explain what happens at the time of death. The heart stops, the brain ceases to function, the blood no longer circulates and cells stop dividing. And in that way we explain death. But what has happened to the person?

What has happened to the one who has now entered a world which is closed to us?

No one returns to explain it to us. No one comes back and says, "It's like this on the other side." And so we have strange thoughts about the state of consciousness of our loved one. We ask ourselves, "How does he feel now? Can he see us or hear us? Will he be aware of the presence of others?" And I think all of us question: "What's it like to die? What is this experience we call death?"

And throughout the history of the world there has never been a complete answer given by man. It's still the same mystery that it always has been since the first man fell to earth in death. Someone went to him and discovered that there was no breath, no heartbeat, and for a better word they called it "death." But it remains a mystery. It is that which is not explainable by man.

But to say that it is a mystery to man, to say that we do not understand it is not to say it is a mystery to God. You know that when one writes a mystery story, the author usually knows the outcome before he begins putting words on paper. The reader may not know the outcome until he has completed his reading but the author has not only solved the mystery but created it in the first place.

And so it is with life. The Author of life, the Creator of each human being, already knows the end of the story. Even if you and I cannot solve it, even if no one in all history can fathom the riddle of death, God knows all about it! There was One who did return from the grave, not to tell us specifically what was on the other side but to show us that Someone did know what was there. Lazarus didn't say anything about his experience in death. But Jesus tried to tell us, "Even if you don't understand about death, I do. I've been there and I've come back to take you through death with me. Come," he says, "and let me take you through. I'll show you the way."

It's a bit like people who have lived the length of their lives in a cave. They have felt their way around the walls, and it's been damp and cold and they know nothing but the darkness. Then someone comes into the cave and says, "Let me take you to a better place, where there are warm breezes and where there is light. There you can see and you can know life much better than you do now."

And the people question him: "What is light?" They do not understand.

The answer comes, "You can't understand it now because you don't know what is outside the cave. But just believe me, it's more wonderful and beautiful than you can possibly imagine."

Then they want to know, "How do we get there?"

And the answer is: "Just follow me. I've been there. I know the way. Just follow me."

That's the way of the Christian, the man of faith. That's the way of the man who believes, as did Paul and Peter and Luther and Will O., whose life we remember today. "I have kept the faith."

Nothing else is so important. The specific events in a man's life cannot be as important as this one statement, said at the time of a man's death: "I have kept the faith."

We noted in the obituary reading that Will received the faith as an infant. God gave faith to him. He was taken by his parents to receive the Sacrament of Holy Baptism in the parish church in his native Germany. It is what God does and not what man does that is important there. It was a gift. Faith has to be just that, because we can't create it. It cannot be earned, and Will O. knew that. The mercy and grace of God gives life.

I have said a number of times that farmers know better than others how much we rely on the gifts of God. "He has given and still preserves my body and soul with all their powers." The closeness of the Creator is evident to most farmers. I believe people who live in concrete cities somehow are separated from the soil and the wind and the rain and they do not understand this quite so much. But Will was a farmer, and as in all of life, he knew first of all that which he received from God. He took what God gave, and God had given him faith.

Will also grew in this faith. No one can stop growth. There will be growth in one direction or another, either in faith or away from it. Will grew within the faith. When the Word of God was preached in this congregation, he was present to hear it. In his home, as I have seen it, the Bible was well-worn and copiously marked. He frequently received Christ himself in the Holy Eucharist. He served this congregation on its governing board.

He taught his family the faith he had received, and through that he grew. He prepared his oldest daughter for death following an accident, and through that he grew. His sons are leaders in the congregation he served. He believed in Christ and continued to believe, and through that he grew in faith.

He had received faith and he had grown in faith. But in the classroom, the proof of a student's knowledge after the course is over is the final exam. And in that, too, we believe Will O. was firm. He finished in faith.

And really there's little more to be said. In this translation from life, through death, into life, there will be no more finishing marks, and the word we use for that is "eternity." In the presence of the eternal God there is life of the highest order. Will has finished in the faith which he received and through which he grew.

Death is a mystery, as we said at the beginning. But it is a mystery only to those without faith, because faith removes doubt and fear. Will O. showed us, through his example, that Paul's words could apply just as well to him: "I have fought the good fight, I have finished the race, I have kept the faith."

We are grateful for the example that Will gave to us of one growing in faith. We pray for his complete reward in the presence of God. Praise God for solving for us, through faith, the greatest mystery of life.

THE PREACHER—James R. Otterness was born in Brookings, South Dakota. He is a graduate of South Dakota State University and Luther Seminary. He has served as pastor of Philip parish in western South Dakota, Our Savior's Church, Omaha, Nebraska, and Lutheran Church of the Risen Lord, Odessa, Texas, where he is still pastor.

THE OCCASION—The sermon was preached for the death of a war veteran who died after a year of poor health.

THE COMMENTS—The sermon has a very personal appeal. It is a sermon within a sermon and the deceased comes close to preaching for his own funeral. Not many opportunities like this occur for the minister, but he is wise to take advantage of them whenever possible.

Truly,
Blessings Are Disguised

"We know that in everything God works for good with those who love him, who are called according to his purpose."   Romans 8:28

It is not easy to preach at the funeral of a close friend. Ellis was my friend. He did a lot of work around the church building with his family. He said he thought the church property ought to look more like heaven than like hell. Ellis found it easier to work with things than with people, even though he was a teacher. He sought for excellence in all that he did and he had little patience with people who did not seek for excellence. He confessed to me that this was one of his sins and he had to struggle with it.

The reason I chose this text from Romans is that Ellis chose it as the basis of an article he once wrote, entitled "Truly, Blessings Are Disguised." I would like to read parts of this article for you.

"I shall relate to you a G.I. story in which these words play a part. The events which so nicely illustrate this Bible verse are the personal experiences of a young man whom I know very well.

"This young man came from a fine Christian home. He was fortunate in being born to his religion because his way to salvation was clearly marked. In his case though, as in many others, things which are gained without effort are seldom appreciated. Still, he attended church services regularly and was a true believer in every sense of the word.

"Then came the great event—his entry in the armed services. It was a time of tremendous international chaos and revolution which threatened to engulf the free peoples of the earth in a maelstrom of fascism and slavery.

"Cognizant of this fact, this individual voluntarily enlisted in that branch of the service to which he thought he could contribute most. Thousands of other idealists, following the same reasoning, also elected to serve in the air corps.

"Perhaps, like these thousands, he was enticed by the visions of earthly gain, silver wings and gold bars! Then, too, young men are spurred on to great achievements by various symbols of success and ability. The hero instinct is a very real part of their person and they are goaded on by the thought of future cheers and applause by an audience composed of fellow countrymen. He, too, had that craving for social recognition and the path to that objective seemed unhampered.

"At the time of his enlistment, there were two induction stations for the air forces, one in his hometown and the other several thousand miles away. Instead of being held at the field near home, he was sent to the distant one to receive preliminary training. The feeling of frustration, however, was gradually displaced by the ever-recurring picture of success. Yet, in moments of meditation, he wondered why he was sent so far to receive a training which might have been more conveniently received close to home.

"Shortly after his instruction began, he was eliminated from the flying training which represented the one great ambition of his life. If we had been able to look within, to view the confused emotions and griefs he endured at that time, we would have been amazed at the extent of his depression. Nothing seemed to matter any longer! His deflated ego would admit of no alternative field. His interest in anything remotely pertaining to the air corps was summarily annihilated. No parents near to offer encouragement, no brother or sister to turn to, dreams shattered, spirit gone, what was the use?

"Until this time his prayers were more or less a matter of lip service. They were offered as a matter of habit, the result of the teachings of his youth. Churchgoing, similarly, was only a matter of form and social custom. The words of Christ held no special meaning for him and his need of the Lord was only a remote possibility. It is indeed a peculiar characteristic of humans in general that in time of peace and plenty they are far from the Lord. As soon as troubled times appear on the horizon, however, these same humans will rush to church in frantic supplication.

"This young man was one of these. Growing out of his misfortune, though, was the earnestness which is lacking in so many of us. His prayers became a refuge, a bulwark against all worldly problems. No longer were they a lip service but the tremendously heartfelt petitions of a dejected human being. The comforting words of Jesus slowly assumed a new significance."

By now, those of you who knew him know that Ellis was writing these words about himself. He goes on to tell of further disappointments, and how these brought him closer to his Lord. He concludes with these words:

"The results of these unhappy incidents had a far-reaching effect. Without them, he might never have been drawn so close to his Lord and Savior. Adversity is a powerful influence in directing us to seek divine aid. That aid, in the last analysis, is the only staple entity in a life of kaleidoscopic changeableness, the one rock we cling to under any circumstances that life and living can bring forth."

Ellis found this same help in his last days when he had to give up working because of blindness. He could not see, but his eyes wept tears and he told me how grateful he was for the wonderful message of the Bible that his wife had been reading to him. He thanked God that so many people had prayed for his recovery and were still praying for him. He had learned to face up to adversity and reality by the grace of God.

Ellis knew he was a sinner, but he also knew he was a forgiven sinner. He knew that the promises of God were valid for him, and that they would also be valid for his family and all of us. I have gone through the experience of the death of my own father when I was very young and I know these promises are true.

We rejoice that Jesus Christ faced up to the imper-

fectness of life in this world and to the reality of un-
timely death, so that by his resurrection we know that
all things work together for good to them that love
God. Death is the ultimate adversity, but we have victory over death in Jesus Christ our Lord.

THE PREACHER—Richard Rehfeldt was born in Appleton, Wisconsin. He is a graduate of the University of Wisconsin and of Wartburg Seminary and has earned a Ph.D. from the University of St. Andrews in Scotland. He has served as pastor at St. Paul, Waverly, Iowa, and at present is pastor at Windsor Heights Lutheran Church, Des Moines, Iowa.

THE OCCASION—The sermon was preached at the funeral of a woman who died suddenly at the age of 51. The family had suffered a number of troubles and reverses previous to this sudden death.

THE COMMENTS—Sudden death is always difficult to deal with. There is no time before death for the mind to make adjustments, no consolation that at least someone has been delivered from pain and suffering. The preacher here wisely makes no explanations but simply points to the comfort from Scripture. The sermon presents only one idea—God still cares for you.

God Cares

Cast all your anxieties on him, for he cares about you.
                                                1 Peter 5:7

Friends in Christ Jesus, we come to this hour, this day with heavy hearts. Only you and God know the extent of your sorrow. Only you and God know the anguish you feel.

Therefore it is right that we turn to the Word of God, for God alone can speak to our hearts in this time of sorrow and sadness. Let me read to you a word found in the pages of the New Testament, a word written in the first letter of Peter: "Cast all your anxieties on him, for he cares about you."

The anxieties, the hurt, the pain, the sorrow you feel, you can cast on the Lord "for he cares about you." If you had to shoulder all this by yourself, you would surely break under the weight of it all. But since you can come to the Lord at his invitation, you can find Someone to carry this burden for you.

This is the message of God to his people throughout the pages of Scripture. The psalmist of old wrote: "Cast your burden on the Lord and he will sustain you" (Ps. 55:22). The Lord Jesus spoke these words: "Come unto me all you that labor and are heavy laden, and I will give you rest" (Matt. 11:28).

"Cast your burden on the Lord. . . ." "Cast your anxieties on him. . . ." "Come unto me. . . ." These are the words of a loving God who invites you to come to him with your burdens. In this moment you can accept that invitation. You can come to him and receive from him strength and comfort for your lives.

Thousands upon thousands down through the ages have done so and have gained a strength and support that has sustained them. When the missionary David Livingstone returned home to Scotland after sixteen years in the jungles of Africa, a group of students at Glasgow University asked: "Mr. Livingstone, what sustained you amidst the toil and hardship and loneliness of your exiled life in the jungle?" David Livingstone replied: "It was the promise, 'Lo, I am with you always, even unto the end.'"

Christian friends, this promise can support us too because we also know that God will be with us always. That is the message of Easter. Not even death itself shall keep us from our Lord. As the Apostle Paul put it: "What can separate us from the love of Christ? Can affliction and hardship?" "I am convinced that there is nothing . . . nothing in all creation that can separate us from the love of God in Christ Jesus our Lord (Rom. 8:38 NEB).

Family of M., look into your own life and see this truth repeated. In past years your family has experienced much sorrow and tragedy. Now you have experienced the sudden death of your loved one. In the face of this, what can we say? We cannot explain it. We can give no reasons for it. But this we can say, even in the midst of tragedy and sudden death, the love of our Lord still reaches down into our lives to sustain and support us.

What gave M. the power to go on in the face of sorrows and hardships? Surely, as she once told me, her strength and ability to carry on were not within herself but came from a source far stronger than she. Today our heavenly Father can grant that same strength to us. So let us, too, "cast our burdens on him." For the God and Father of our Lord Jesus Christ cares for us.

I know that in the days when we are face to face with a sudden and unexpected death, we find it hard to accept the fact that God cares for us. But God never promised us freedom from sorrow and tragedy, from pain and hurt, from disease and death. Yet God did promise us power and victory *over* sorrow and tragedy, pain and hurt, disease and death. The God who did not spare even his Son, but sent him to this earth for us, the God who allowed his only Son to suffer death on a cross for each of us—*that* God cares for us!

A moment ago we sang *In the Cross of Christ I Glory.* That was a favorite of M.'s. The reason is clear. In that cross of Calvary she and others like her saw a loving God lay down his life for us. The cross of Calvary is the supreme example of the fact that God cares for us. As the hymn writer put it:

> In the Cross of Christ I glory,
> Towering o'er the wrecks of time;
> All the light of sacred story
> Gathers round its head sublime.

When the woes of life o'ertake me,
Hopes deceive and fears annoy,
Never shall the Cross forsake me;
Lo! it glows with peace and joy.

SBH 64

Dear friends, we shall never understand why things in life happen as they do. We shall never understand on this side of heaven. Yet one thing we *do* know and understand. God cares for us. The cross is the symbol of our loving, caring God. So in this hour, in this day, and in the hours and days to come, cling to the one who hung on that cross, knowing that you can "cast your anxieties on him, for he cares about you."

Remember, our Lord Jesus has promised to uphold you with his strength in this life. Above all, our crucified and risen Lord has promised to all who believe in him, eternal life in his heavenly kingdom.

THE PREACHER—Otto Reitz is a native of Fairfield, Washington. He is a graduate of Pacific Lutheran University and of Wartburg Seminary. He has served parishes in Shell Rock, Iowa, Janesville, Wisconsin, and Graettinger, Iowa, where he is currently pastor of Bethel Lutheran Church.

THE OCCASION—The sermon was preached at the funeral of a man who had suffered for almost half of his life from crippling arthritis.

THE COMMENTS—There is a poetic rhythm to the sermon. The preacher uses a great deal of textual material but it is cleverly interwoven into the sermon. The congregation probably wasn't always aware when the minister was quoting Scripture and when he was commenting on it. The sermon deals delicately with the weaknesses of the sufferer but the strongest stress is on the assurances God gives us.

Let All
God's People Say Amen

Blessed be the Lord, the God of Israel, from everlasting to everlasting! And let all the people say, "Amen!" Praise the Lord.   Psalm 106:48

When the word "Amen" was spoken, C. passed away. After brief devotions, it seemed as if C. waited until the word "Amen" was spoken and then he passed away.

This psalm verse therefore seems a fitting one for us to use today, especially the words, "Let all the people say, 'Amen.'"

Amen, first of all, to suffering completed. The Psalmist tells us, "Blessed be the Lord, the God of Israel, from everlasting to everlasting! And let all the people say, 'Amen!' Praise the Lord!"

Let all the people say Amen. This was, no doubt, a part of their liturgy. The leader urged the people to state their acceptance of the prayer and praise that was spoken by adding the word Amen. It was their agreement with, their acceptance of what had been spoken.

The Amen of our text occurs at the close of a psalm. This psalm recounts many of the things that had happened to the people of Israel—their deliverance from Egypt, their long and difficult journey through the desert, and their arrival in the land of Canaan. But in this land they also experienced troubles. They sinned, says the Psalmist. "Then the anger of the Lord was kindled against his people . . . and they were brought low in their iniquity. Nevertheless (the Lord) regarded their distress, when he heard their cry. He remembered for their sake his covenant, and relented according to the abundance of his steadfast love. And so all the people said, 'Amen,' Praise the Lord!"

Let all God's people say Amen. Amen to suffering completed. So it was for C. when he passed away. Amen, it's all over now. Amen, it's ended. Amen, no more pain and anguish and discomfort. Through more than half the years of his life C. suffered from crippling arthritis. The recurring stabs of pain. The immobility. The necessity of depending on others. But now it's all over. It's ended, the wheelchair, the walker, the cortisone, the aspirins. It's all over. Let all God's people say Amen to suffering completed.

I read recently the story of eighteen-year-old Eric Ryback who was the first person to hike the Pacific Crest Trail along the mountains from Canada to Mexico. He had a pretty hard time of it. And once when he stopped to telephone his folks and tell them all his woes, they ended the conversation with encouraging words about "improving conditions" and how it's good "to suffer a little."

Is it good to suffer a little? The Bible says, "He whom the Lord loves he chastens." It tells us that "we must, through many tribulations, enter the kingdom of heaven." Peter writes: "In this you rejoice, though now for a little while you may have to suffer various trials so that the genuineness of your faith, more precious than gold which though perishable, is tested by fire, may redound to praise and glory and honor at the revelation of Jesus Christ."

God does sometimes allow suffering to enter our lives for our good. It is the Christian's confidence that God can use even these difficulties to bring about a positive result. We know that he used Christ's suffering. Jesus endured many hardships—birth in a manger, life among the poor and finally execution upon a cross. Yet God used all this to win salvation for us.

And so we know that

> Whate'er our God ordains is right;
> He never will deceive me;
> He leads me by the proper path;
> I know he will not leave me.
> I take, content,
> What he hath sent;
> His hand can turn my griefs away,
> (So) patiently I wait his day.

But finally there comes a day when God says to sickness and pain and tears, "Thus far and no farther." "He regarded his people's distress when he heard their cry." And he heard the cry of C. also. Let all God's people say Amen. For in heaven God himself will "wipe away every tear from his people's eyes, and death shall be no more for them, neither shall there be mourning nor crying nor pain anymore, for these former things have passed away."

And now let us say Amen for God's grace and goodness. "Blessed be the Lord, the God of Israel, from everlasting to everlasting! And let all the people say,

'Amen.' " Yes, they agreed. They accepted God's goodness. They opened their hands to receive his forgiveness and his pardon.

A large part of this psalm recounts the sins of God's people. "Both we and our fathers have sinned," says the psalmist. "We have committed iniquity, we have done wickedly." The people soon forgot God's great deeds for them. They did not wait for his counsel. They grumbled in the desert. They made a golden calf and worshiped it. Then they despised the pleasant land God gave them. They even sacrificed to the idols of Canaan.

Yet, wonder of wonders, when they repented of their sins and cried to God of his mercy, "He remembered for their sake his covenant, and relented according to the abundance of his steadfast love." He is a God of grace and mercy. No wonder the psalmist says, "Blessed be the Lord the God of Israel . . . and let all the people say, 'Amen.' " Let them say Amen to God's grace and goodness. Amen, yes we accept it. Amen, yes we rejoice in it. Amen, yes we believe in this God and claim his salvation.

So it was for C. It isn't honest at a funeral only to praise the departed. We all have sinned and fallen short of the glory of God. And C. did too, and he knew it. He was often abrupt with others, perhaps as a cover-up for his physical disabilities. But in recent months I saw another side of C. He had an almost childlike faith and was eager to receive God's grace and forgiveness. I witnessed this again just a week ago when he received Holy Communion. Amen he was saying, and he said it when he died at the close of a prayer. Amen to God's grace and goodness.

And Amen lastly to eternal blessings. "Save us, O Lord our God," prayed the psalmist. And God did and he still does. He brought his people home from the land of bondage and promised them eternal blessings. "Let all the people say Amen to this."

The bitter poet who wrote the poem *Invictus* begins with the cry: "Out of the night that covers me, black as the Pit from pole to pole." And so he dwells in darkness and despair. But these are not the Christian's feelings. The child of God looks forward with confident hope to be "forever with the Lord." Because Jesus rose from the dead victorious, we too shall live forever with him.

A few years ago archaeologists opened the centuries-old sarcophagus of one of the pharaohs of Egypt. The first man to enter the tomb saw the gold and jewels and articles of beauty, and he was struck dumb by the magnificence of it all. Finally his companions outside demanded to know whether he could see anything. Whereupon he whispered back, "Yes, wonderful things."

What is there beyond the grave? Do you see anything on the other side of death? Yes, answers our Lord who has gone on ahead of us. Wonderful things. So wonderful that we can't even imagine how magnificent it is. Therefore, says a poet,

> Grow old along with me. The best is yet to be,
> The last of life, for which the first was made;
> Our times are in His hand, who saith, 'A whole I planned,
> Youth shows but half; trust God, see all, nor be afraid.'

And to this let all God's people say Amen evermore.

THE PREACHER—John Thomas Rotto is a native of Minneapolis. He is a graduate of Luther College and Luther Seminary. He has served parishes in Fairfax, California, in Forman, Rutland, and Valley City, North Dakota, and at present is pastor of United Lutheran Church, Grand Forks, North Dakota.

THE OCCASION—The sermon was preached at the death of a 91-year-old lady who had been a charter member of the church from which she was buried. She was well known in the community and everyone called her Grandma.

THE COMMENTS—The preacher uses an Old Testament text but gives it a New Testament emphasis. The sermon is remarkable for the interpretation it puts on age, particularly the stress on what this says to younger people. There is a good idea here for every preacher who must preach at the death of an aged Christian.

Precious in His Sight

Precious in the sight of the Lord is the death of his saints.   Psalm 116:15

Dear fellow Christians. While Grandma S. lived, there was one descriptive word that came to me after every visit with her. The word was "precious."

Others of you used this word about her also. I've heard many of you say, "Isn't she precious?" The words denote that we thought her of great value to us, it was good to know her, good to be in her presence. Her children and grandchildren sensed this. Her peers and the neighborhood kids thought so too. This is why today there is a passage of Scripture that will not leave my mind, a verse from the 116th Psalm. "Precious in the sight of the Lord is the death of his saints."

Of course, there is really no measure of value placed on any of God's children, in the sense that one has more value than another. The value his saints have is never more, never less than the precious worth of the innocent sufferings and death and the shed blood of Jesus our Lord.

All life is of value in the sight of God, but precious when it has been bathed in the blood of Jesus Christ.

121

No death is precious in the sight of the Lord unless that death is the death of a saint. And a saint is a person who is a sinner but who daily bathes in the waters of Baptism and is daily forgiven and receives new life and status as a saint by our gracious God. This is why the psalmist can say, "Precious in the sight of the Lord is the death of his saints." They are precious in death because they have been precious in life!

We're talking, really, about the gift God gives us in Holy Baptism. We become his precious children, precious to God from the moment of Baptism on through life. We are precious because we are the recipients of a precious gift.

We are children of God our parent. A very real analogy is this: just as a child is precious to parents because the child is the receiver and object of affection and care in evil days and good, in sickness and in health, when naughty and when nice, so also God regards his children as precious even though they are weak and sinful, and often err from the parental path.

The saint of God is precious in death because in life God regards him or her as a valuable servant. God values the labors of the saints, the good they do, the example they set, the witness they give by daily life and speech to others in the church and to those outside the church.

Here also in the glory of living long. They are precious in long life. Precious to God because their old age is a testimony to all of us of God's goodness that has not failed them even though they lived long beyond the ordinary life span of human beings.

This ought to speak loudly to those of us who are

younger. We so often feel that life is tough, that it is hard to hang on to our faith, that it is often a burden to be faithful in Sunday worship, a pain to get the kids to Sunday school and we wonder if it is worth it in the long run to try to stick close to Christ in word and sacrament. Yet the testimony of the precious saint whom the Lord permits to live long among us is just this—God is powerful and strong. When Scripture says, "He is able to save to the uttermost," it means God is able to hang on to us through thick and thin.

The encouragement that a long life like Grandma's brings to us who are young is this—if God is able to hold this old person as his own, if he is able through many long years, through hardship and suffering such as we perhaps will never experience, then surely he will be able to hold us fast in the faith.

But there is a secret to the preciousness of these long-lived saints. There are certain cherished times that they never permitted to be stolen from them and that are necessary if you and I are to be able to die precious in the sight of the Lord.

These cherished times were their appointments with Jesus Christ! They faithfully kept, they never let themselves stray very far from the hearing and preaching of God's Word and the receiving of Holy Communion where they knew Christ had arranged to meet them in his special ways. Many times I have marveled to see how hungry people like Grandma become for the word and the sacraments. They hunger for these means of grace not because they think they are holy and saintly, but because they know they are sinners and tell me so as their pastor. They seem to need more than anything else God's reassuring word and his reassuring touch through the bread and wine of Holy Communion.

There is something grandly victorious about the death of God's saints. Their death speaks loudly that God is God. That God's Son is indeed God's Son. The death of the saints is always a "little Easter." It is not Christ rising from the dead after battling with the prince of darkness, but instead, people such as you and I moving from the battlefields of this planet into the safety of Christ's holy city. It's continuing life that we celebrate today.

St. John has recorded for us his vision of the throne room of heaven. He tells us that he saw a great multitude robed in white standing before the throne. To the question: "Who are these who are arrayed in white robes and where do they come from?" there is the answer:

> These are they who have come out of the great tribulation, they have washed their robes and made them white in the blood of the lamb, therefore are they before the throne of God, and serve him day and night within his temple: and he who sits upon the throne will shelter them with his presence. They shall hunger no more, neither thirst any more; the sun shall not strike them, nor any scorching heat, For the lamb in the midst of the throne will guide them to springs of living water and God will wipe away every tear from their eyes.

And so we say with the psalmist, "Precious in the sight of the Lord is the death of his saints!" Precious because their death is not death but life through faith in our Lord, Jesus Christ.

THE PREACHER—Alvin C. Rueter was born in Parkers Prairie, Minnesota. He is a graduate of Dana College, Blair, Nebraska, Lutheran Seminary, Columbus, Ohio, and the University of Minnesota. He has served as pastor of Christ Church, Monterey Park, California, Chapel of Peace, Inglewood, California, Bethany in Tulsa, American in Lincoln, Nebraska, and at present is pastor of Bethlehem-in-the-Midway, St. Paul. He is also instructor in homiletics at Luther Seminary.

THE OCCASION—The sermon was preached at the death of an aged man who had no church connections although his wife was a church member. He was not opposed to the church but had no interest in joining.

THE COMMENTS—The preacher here does the proper thing under the circumstances. He finds some good things to say about the deceased but makes no judgment. Then he turns to the subject of pain and applies to the living the comfort of the gospel.

The God of All Comfort

Blessed be the God and Father of our Lord Jesus Christ, the Father of all mercies and God of all comfort, who comforts us in all our affliction. 2 Corinthians 1:3-4a

An important link in our chain of neighborhood relationships has been removed. A husband is gone. Even though he suffered severely for several years and even though he took a lot of work and care, we just can't deny the heartache. The loss extends beyond your home and the houses on your street to others to whom he'd become a father or a grandfather. The loss will also be felt by those who came to visit him, to whom he was a most interesting conversationalist. He had skilled fingers and an active mind as we can see from his vocation of servicing microscopes and his hobby with model trains. There is good reason to be sad.

We turn to our God for comfort. There are several verses in the first chapter of second Corinthians that I wish to use for my text: "Blessed be the God and Father of our Lord Jesus Christ, the Father of mercies and God of all comfort, who comforts us in all our affliction."

The God of all comfort! Those words immediately cause us to ask: "Why is there suffering in the world?"

And I can't answer that question. The reason for cancer, what causes children to be born with handicaps, why are there tears at all?—I simply don't know. Many people, myself included, have puzzled about the pain in the world and have tried to fathom the mystery. Some attempts at a solution make pretty good sense, but when you come up against the ultimate question, "Why does a good God permit any pain at all?" there simply isn't any total answer.

The text, however, says that the God of all comfort is "the Father of our Lord Jesus Christ." We see the father in the son. Jesus once said, "He who has seen me has seen the Father" (John 14:9). When we look at Jesus, we see that the Father of mercies has shared our pain. Our Lord was as poor as anyone. He was even a refugee, fleeing for his life with his parents when no more than two years old. He worked for his living as a carpenter. Then he became a professional teacher. According to worldly eyes he would be judged a failure because he lasted only three years as a rabbi and then— as though he were a common criminal—he underwent gruesome execution.

So whenever we probe and search for the cause of our grief, whenever we're tempted to blame God for our troubles, we bump into this most peculiar thing, that God suffers too. And this very tendency of ours, to blame God for everything that goes wrong—he has accommodated himself to it, he allowed himself to become our scapegoat.

"The Lord has laid on him the iniquity of us all" (Isa. 53:6).

"For our sake he made him to be sin who knew no sin, so that in him we might become the righteousness of God" (2 Cor. 5:21).

If we see the world as unfriendly, he surely found it that way too.

Yet looking at the life of Jesus, we find no grounds for concluding that God must be hostile. Even when the world made no bones about trying to get rid of him, he wouldn't stay in the tomb. To a world so hostile that it claims God is hostile, he came back. To offer grace and love, peace and forgiveness, Jesus still keeps coming back.

So whenever we're puzzled by the problem of pain, we remind ourselves that he's the Father of our Lord Jesus Christ, and that though we can't fully unravel every strand of the mystery of suffering, we do cling to the God who shares our suffering. That's how he "comforts us in all our afflictions."

Our hearts go out to you, Mrs. ————. We trust that our common faith in the Father of mercies and the God of all comfort will sustain you and us in the days and weeks ahead.

THE PREACHER—Stanley D. Schneider was born in Massillon, Ohio. He is a graduate of Capital University and of Lutheran Theological Seminary. He has studied at the University of St. Andrews, Scotland, and the Ecumenical Institute, Geneva. He has served as pastor of Christ Church, Regina, Saskatchewan, St. Paul's, Toledo, and St. Paul's, Michigan City, Indiana. He was Professor of Homiletics at Lutheran Theological Seminary in Columbus, Ohio, for a number of years. At present he is again pastor at St. Paul's in Toledo.

THE OCCASION — Three young children were playing around a grain elevator. The oldest, a girl, slipped and fell to her death. The family was unchurched but requested a seminary student to find them a preacher for the girl's funeral.

THE COMMENTS—The situation is doubly difficult since the death is so unexpected and tragic and the family is unknown to the preacher. The sermon is simple and clear. Deep theological content would have been out of place on such an occasion. Note that here the preacher preaches to his text and presents it at the very end of the sermon.

Sharing

Have no anxiety about anything but in everything by prayer and supplication with thanksgiving let your requests be made known to God. And the peace of God which passes all understanding will keep your hearts and minds in Christ Jesus.   Philippians 4:6-7

Most of you here do not know me. I am a professor of theology who teaches at a seminary. Today I am in a situation more often faced by parish pastors than by theological professors.

But I am not here as a professor. I am simply here as a Christian person to share. I am here to share your grief. I am here to share God's grace. As I said, I am not here as a professor, and I guess I couldn't be in some ways. One of the questions that professors are often asked is, "Why?" We are expected to come up with answers to that sort of question.

In one form or another that question is being asked now, "Why?" I need not finish it, for each one finishes it in his or her own way.

"Why?" I cannot answer it. I can only share it, because I ask it too. I do not know the answer. When a child dies too soon, when there is an accident, we ask,

131

"Why?"—perhaps thinking that if we knew some sort of an answer, the comfort of understanding would be ours.

But I can't offer that, because I don't have the answer. I share your grief, grief that needs no more words from me, because it is too difficult to express.

If no answers, what then? I share your grief and God's grace. I don't know the answers but I know the one who does, and that is God.

He may not give you the answer, the comfort of understanding. But he will offer you the strength of faith, in believing that he is here, and there, and everywhere.

He once came here in Jesus Christ. Jesus is the best picture that I have of God. From what I know about Jesus, I can say this. What has happened that brings us here is not an act of God, nor is it his will.

When Jesus was here he healed the sick; he raised to life a little girl and the son of a widow. Quite clearly Jesus did not think of accidents, sickness, illness and death as the will of God. He thought of them as the reverse of that will. These were among the very things he had come to help and to overcome.

What then can be said at a time like this? I can say that God is as grieved as we are, that he is sharing our sorrow and our grief. His heart is reaching out to meet our hearts. That is what we call grace.

I also believe that he has it in his power to make it up to those who seem to us to be taken away too soon, and to those to whom sorrow and suffering has tragically come.

If God is love, I am certain that there is more to life than this, that great as grief is, grace is greater. In the part of life that God has in store for us a life cut off too soon can go on. Lives that are touched by tragedy can also find strength to go on.

I shall not try to pretend to explain sorrow. I have to say, "I don't know why this has happened." But I also have to say that God knows and loves and forgives and gives.

You may not understand that either. There is much that is beyond understanding. That suggests the word that I would leave with you. A man named Paul wrote it. He knew God too. This is what he wrote:

> Have no anxiety about anything, but in everything by prayer and supplication with thanksgiving let your requests be made known to God. And the peace of God which passes all understanding will keep your hearts and minds in Christ Jesus (Phil. 4:6-7).

THE PREACHER—Mark Thomsen was born in Owatonna, Minnesota. He is a graduate of Dana College and Trinity Seminary, Blair, Nebraska. He earned a Master of Theology degree at Princeton Seminary and a Ph.D. at Northwestern University and Garrett Theological Seminary. He has served as missionary to Nigeria, campus pastor at the University of Northern Iowa, faculty member at Dana College and at present is pastor of St. Peter Lutheran Church, Dubuque, Iowa.

THE OCCASION—The sermon was preached at the funeral of a three-year-old girl who, while playing in a neighbor's driveway, was run over by a truck driven by another neighbor. The parents were heartbroken by the tragedy, and family and friends painfully and angrily asked how a good God could allow the life of this beautiful little girl to be so senselessly destroyed.

THE COMMENTS—The preacher faces the problem honestly and does the only thing possible under the circumstances—he turns to Scripture and stresses what we do know rather than trying to explain what must remain a mystery. He uses two texts since no single passage deals adequately with the situation. The sermon is short and employs no ornament or fancy language.

Jesus Shares Your Grief

Words at times seem inadequate and meaningless, and I do not have many words to share with you today. But I would like to remind you of two stories from the life of Jesus which reveal that Jesus *shares* your tears and your agonizing questions.

The gospel of John relates that one of Jesus' good friends, Lazarus, had died. When Jesus arrived at Lazarus' home in Bethany, he was met by the sisters of Lazarus—Martha and Mary. There is a beautiful description of this encounter which includes these words:

> When Mary arrived where Jesus was and saw him, she fell at his feet. "Lord," she said, "if you had been here, my brother would not have died!" Jesus saw her weeping, and the Jews who had come with her weeping, also; *his heart was touched and he was deeply moved.* "Where have they buried him?" he asked them. "Come and see, Lord," they answered. Jesus wept (John 11:32-36).

Jesus wept. That story from the life of Jesus is a promise that you do not bear your grief, your deep sorrow, and your tears alone. Jesus *shares* them with you. And because he is that Son of God in whom we see the

Eternal Father, we know and trust that God himself weeps with you and us today. That faith does not take the suffering and the heartache away. It does not erase the pain and the tears at the loss of a precious and beautiful little girl, and it shouldn't. But it is a promise that God walks with you through the valley of the shadow of death; he weeps with you there, and he has you in his hands.

But in anguish we say, "Kelly was so small and so beautiful. Kelly had so much ahead of her. Why was her life taken away? What kind of God allows cruel and senseless deaths like Kelly's?" How do you answer questions like that in the midst of pain and grief? There are times in our life when we have no certain answers to the tragic questions of life. Jesus himself shared that experience of ours. As he hung dying on the cross which was planted in the hill called Golgotha, he himself cried out to his Father: "My God, my God, why have you forsaken me?" (Mark 15:34).

Jesus trusted that he had walked his Father's way. He knew that his death was part of God's will for him, but he didn't understand why it had to be that way and why he was so all alone. In his pain and in his loneliness he cried out in the darkness of that windswept hill, "My God, my God, why have you forsaken me?" We cry out in the darkness of Kelly's death, but as we do, we can trust that our heavenly Father understands our bewilderment, our tragic cries, our questions. God holds you and loves you in the darkness of loss and grief and questions.

One final word. Jesus who shares your tears and questions is also the Jesus who called to Lazarus, "Lazarus, come forth!" and in so doing raised him from the dead. This is also the same Jesus who promises: "Let not your hearts be troubled; believe in God, believe also in me. In my Father's house are many rooms; if it were not so, would I have told you that I go to prepare a place for you?" (John 14:1-2).

Above all, this is Jesus who was not ultimately forsaken and left alone on Golgotha, for God raised him from the dead. Through the power of his Father, Jesus calls back to you and to us today from beyond death and dying, "Kelly's with me and she is okay."

THE PREACHER—Wayne Weissenbuehler was born in Charles City, Iowa. He is a graduate of Wartburg College and Wartburg Seminary. He began his ministry at St. John's in Pittsburg, Kansas, and also served at Christ the King, Denver. He is now an assistant to the president of the Central District of The American Lutheran Church.

THE OCCASION—The sermon was preached at a service marking the death of a man 58 years old who died very suddenly. He had been a very active member of the local congregation.

THE COMMENTS—The sermon is dominated by the spirit of the pastor. You feel that he does care, that he is truly concerned for those who mourn. Often this is more important than the specific words that are spoken. Nothing is more upsetting than a perfunctory funeral sermon. The illustration close to the end of the message is a good one and worth borrowing.

God Says Yes

For the Son of God, Jesus Christ, whom we preached among you . . . was not Yes and No but in him it is always Yes. For all the promises of God find their Yes in him. That is why we utter the Amen through him to the glory of God.   2 Corinthians 1:19-20

When someone for whom you care very much dies, the hurt becomes enormous. When that death comes suddenly, without warning to someone too young, with too many good things ahead of him, to someone who always seemed to make life brighter and better for those around him, the pain easily gives way to anger and a sense of frustration. We feel cheated. When this someone is named Vearn, a man loved and needed by his wife and sons, his job, and his church, our sense of shock gives way to the admission that we have again seen the old enemy death at its worst. Yet I am here to proclaim that in spite of this, death does not have the last word. Jesus Christ does, and his word to our friend Vearn and his word to Bette and to all of us is, Yes. It is okay. All is not lost.

Today it is all right for us to hurt and cry, to be frustrated and angry over our loss and grief. It is a mark of our love. It is a mark of the measure of this man, but there is another word that must be spoken, a word even more true, a word that will keep our hurt from turning into despair and bitterness and will point us to our real hope. This word is the promise of Jesus Christ. "I say to Vearn my Yes forever and I say it also to you. You are mine. I hold you in my hand forever. Death cannot win you because I have died for you and am alive and in me you shall live eternally." Today through our tears and sense of loss, we find our grief softened by the knowledge that his Lord has said Yes to Vearn. A long time ago he said Yes to Delia Voss's son in Baptism. That promise was renewed many times in Holy Communion and then last Friday Vearn cashed in on Jesus' baptismal promise that one day all the old would finally be put to death and the new arise to live before God forever.

I think today we need also to say some things about how God said Yes to Vearn during his life lest we let the hurt of the moment blind us to the great things that happened in his life. He was a neat guy. He loved people and people loved him. He had a streak of orneriness that made him fully alive and fully human and great to have as a friend. He really cared about people and was generous and giving almost to a fault. I can only testify that it was great to be his friend as well as his pastor. He was a friend of unwavering faithfulness and I shall miss him deeply. But all this testifies to how good it was that he was alive and what a good life it was. You and I know it is not how long you live, but how well.

On March 18, 1969, I stood in this pulpit and spoke

about the Voss's son, Mike, who gave his life in Viet
Nam. At that time we talked to Vearn and Bette about
the pride we felt for the way Mike lived and gave his
life. While it could not change his death, it helped us
to see that it was his life that mattered. Now we can
and must say the same thing about Vearn. When Jesus
Christ says Yes to us and when we live in the light of
that Yes, then life is lived as it was meant to be. Today
is the day for each of us to ask about our own faithfulness to the promise spoken to us by God.

A famous preacher once preached the funeral sermon
for his beloved wife with whom he had worked and
lived so closely but who was, like Vearn, snatched away
so suddenly. His theme was, "When life tumbles in,
what then?" I think this would express your feelings,
Bette. We mourn with you but would also say to you
and the boys, to you, his mother, and his family that
Jesus Christ's word to you also is Yes. You can mourn
and hurt and fear but you do not sorrow as those who
have no hope. God is with you and he promises even
in the midst of disaster to give strength and power to
you. I said to you from the beginning, "You will be
okay." I say it again. It is the very promise of your God
who himself endured pain and death in order to go
through it with us and to be near us in our sorrow and
to help us grow in spite of all. He says Yes to you by
surrounding you with family who care and friends
that are the best that anyone could have. You are in
the midst of a church who will support you with the
only strength that wins, the strength of the Holy Spirit.

To me there has always been a center in your many
homes which has made them a warm, open, inviting

place for me and my family. It is the kitchen table. Around that we often celebrated the sacrament of coffee and conversation, spiced with humor, arguments and love. To me it is an apt symbol of the hope that we share of finally one day gathering around God's table in heaven for the day of delight that never ends. Vearn has gone on ahead. That is okay. For by God's grace we all look forward in hope to that day when his Yes is ours forever.

THE PREACHER—William H. Weiblen is a native of Miller, South Dakota. He is a graduate of Wartburg College, Wartburg Seminary, Harvard University and Friedrich Alexander University, Erlangen, Germany. He served parishes in Bryan, Ohio, and Waverly, Iowa, before joining the faculty of Wartburg Seminary. At present he is president of that institution, located in Dubuque, Iowa.

THE OCCASION—The memorial service was conducted for a man who had served as a pastor for only four months after entering the seminary late in life. He died from a sudden heart attack.

THE COMMENTS—The memorial service, held at the seminary sometime after the death, made it possible for the preacher to speak more confidently, since the shock of sudden death had somewhat abated. There is a ring of celebration in the sermon which triumphs over the gloomy facts of death. But it is the promise of eternity which makes this stress possible. The use of personal material also helps here. The preacher should always make the sermon as personal as possible although often he is at a loss in this area.

Celebrating Our Hope

Blessed be the God and Father of our Lord Jesus Christ! By his great mercy we have been born anew to a living hope through the resurrection of Jesus Christ from the dead, and to an inheritance which is imperishable, undefiled, and unfading, kept in heaven for you, who by God's power are guarded through faith for a salvation ready to be revealed in the last time.   1 Peter 1:3-5

For I am sure that neither death, nor life, nor angels, nor principalities, nor things present, nor things to come, nor powers, nor height, nor depth, nor anything else in all creation, will be able to separate us from the love of God in Christ Jesus our Lord.   Romans 8:38-39

This is, indeed, a time to celebrate the unlimited hope, the living hope, to which God has called us in Jesus Christ. We have been born into a new hope. The living hope into which we have been recreated is something that not only calls us to a consummation at the end of all things but is above all a hope that enables us to live now with direction, with meaning, and with significance.

When Karl Thomas wrote his guides and goals for ministry about a year ago, he wrote that he did not understand the pastoral vocation to be something that was qualitatively different from the ministry of all the people of God. Karl stated that, in his mind, being a pastor, though not something better than the calling of every Christian, nevertheless was an integral part of God's design to communicate the gospel and establish the church.

Karl wrote that, as a son of a pastor, he had felt the agitation to become a pastor as long as he could remember. He continued that now that he was about to be assigned to a district of the church and shortly to be called and ordained, he recognized, in a very special way, the completeness of God's grace that had sustained him through his years of service in other vocations before coming to the seminary. Karl said that he looked forward to beginning his new vocation as a pastor in vibrant hope and joyous expectancy because the God of all grace, who had brought him to this point, was at the beginning and end of everything that he sought to do. He concluded his statement of guides and goals with these words: "In my case, whatever time God gives me to serve in whatever way I am called, it will be an exciting and rewarding adventure in faith to which I bring the hope of being utilized and used to a degree never before possible in my experience."

It was the unbounded hope in Jesus Christ which led him to acknowledge his Savior's lordship and to find direction and purpose in life through him. So today, when we think of how quickly the pastoral ministry of Karl Thomas ended, it is well that we remind ourselves of the living hope in which he began that ministry. The unbounded hope which led Karl Thomas to acknowledge that Jesus Christ is Lord and enabled him to find direction and purpose in life is the same hope in which we gather here in this service today. We thank God for such a hope. We thank God for the life of Karl Thomas and for the hope in which that life was lived. Today, in a very special way, we seek God's direction in the face of death, knowing that we have been given a new and living hope.

Death is a very real power. Death strikes with telling force into the lives of each of us. The brutal force of death cannot be minimized. Death is the sobering reality which encounters us at every turn. However, we do not live in the somber, disturbing, all-present power of death alone. There are indeed persons who would tell us that the only way to find meaning when we face death is to accept the reality of death. "Accept death and then throw this acceptance in death's face and in a courageous act to go ahead and make something of the time allotted to you in spite of death." By God's grace and in the power of the hope which grace brings, we can do that and more. We can hold up the reality of life in the face of death because of the resurrection. This memorial service is a time for us to acknowledge the victory of our Lord over death; the victory also in the death of Karl Thomas.

As things turned out, Karl Thomas did not have much time for that pastoral vocation which, as he said, in some ways he was being prepared for throughout his entire life as husband and father, Army officer, business executive before he became pastor of a unique ecumenical parish. And yet the impact that he made in Kimball, South Dakota in those four months of exercising his pastoral vocation was tremendous and lasting. The meaning of it all was brought together very well by one of our graduates, Joel Flugstad, who preached the sermon at his burial service. Joel said, "In our mind the time for Karl was all too short. But who said that the meaning of life is determined in length or in quantity?" So it is that we, too, today need to be reminded of the fact that at a death like Karl's, it isn't the length of time we look at but it is at the wholeness of life as it has been given by God and recreated in the power of the resurrection.

The life we can live by grace is a life in which we can extol the hope into which we have been reborn. Today we can turn from the memorial service with renewed and thankful dedication to the God who calls us from death to life, from sadness to hope, from meaninglessness and lack of direction to purpose and power. We can join with you, Vivian, with you children, Peter, Janet, Patricia, Brenda, and grandchildren, Michael and Pete, in celebrating the grace of our loving Father. We are certain, by the power of the resurrection with Paul, that nothing can separate us from the love of God which is in Christ Jesus. May we rejoice in the hope to which we have been called and may that hope give us the power to live in triumph of life over death.

THE PREACHER—Erling H. Wold was born in Maddock, North Dakota. He is a graduate of Luther College in Decorah, Iowa, of Luther Seminary, St. Paul, and of Chicago Lutheran Seminary. He has served at Trinity, Fort Worth, Texas, Burr Oak, Iowa, Emmanuel, North Hollywood, California, United, Grand Forks, North Dakota. He has served on the staff of Luther College, and at present is pastor of St. Olaf Lutheran Church, Garden Grove, California.

THE OCCASION—The sermon was preached for the death of a father.

THE COMMENTS—The sermon is outstanding in the use of illustrations. The preacher pours them on and the effect drives the message home. Not everyone has so many personal experiences to relate, but such material can be very useful when available.

We Offer You This Jesus

That I may know him and the power of his resurrection, and may share his sufferings, becoming like him in his death, that if possible I may attain the resurrection from the dead.   Philippians 3:10-11

The hearts of all of us that are here with you today at this memorial service for your husband and your father reach out for you. We want to put the arms of our love around you. We want you to know we deeply care.

We hurt with you in the fact that your lives have been shattered by this unwanted death. You know better than we the agony through which you are going. You never asked for this death. You didn't want it. It stalked in, like St. Paul said, as your hated enemy. You dislike this kind of confrontation. You feel deeply hurt.

Death shadows over so much that we do. It comes to threaten us, even in our happiest moments. It destroys relationships. It seems to say to us, "I have you in my clutches. I'm imprisoning you. I have the final word. You may struggle to use all your intellect and all your brilliance in an effort to ward me off. You

151

fondly believe *you* have the ultimate voice but the ultimate voice is mine."

How can we handle death? How can we cope with it? How can we come to grips with it as a grim reality? There are a lot of ways that we've perfected as humans to escape it. For some it's living it up. They cry, "Pluck the rose before you die. Eat, drink and be merry. Let nothing inhibit the moments that you have." With others it's making noise. I've seen people plunge into mad activity just to run away from death's finality and its ultimacy. I've seen others pretend that death isn't real. I sat with one such person in Chicago who had played this game all her life. Suddenly, dying at only thirty-two, she was totally afraid of what the future held for her.

I saw this just as visibly in Madagascar. A funeral cortege was making its way to a grave seven miles down a dusty road. An empty coffin came first, followed by the body some ten feet back. The carriers, gaily clad as if they were living a pretense, kept weaving back and forth from ditch to ditch. I imagine they must have walked three times the normal distance before they finally reached the grave. At that point they quickly deposited their burden and ran. Fearful of evil spirits that might follow them, this was their way of escaping death's reality.

There are some who become angry. Martha and Mary were deeply disturbed when brother Lazarus died. They were visibly angry at Jesus. Nowhere does his kindness glow more clearly than in his acceptance of their hurt.

So we offer you again this Jesus. St. Paul is simply

enamoured of him. His only desire is put so simply: "That I may know him." Somehow all of life is wrapped up in the person of this one who rose from the dead. The beauty of Jesus is not that he offers some "pie in the sky, by and by." The glory of his work on our behalf is that by his cross and resurrection, he destroyed death and provided life as a day-by-day possibility.

I realized this personally in a fantastic way just four years ago. While body surfing, a giant wave upended me and smashed me against the ocean floor. Totally paralyzed, I saw a light brighter than the noonday sun at my right side. Like Paul, I recognized his presence. He was there when I was broken. Jesus never leaves nor forsakes us. You can hang tight to his love. In the center of all our pain stands his presence, caring, loving, self-giving. He whispers to you, "You really belong to me."

Paul makes resurrection reality even more personal when he says, "That I may share the power of his resurrection." This resurrection energy is a present reality. St. John said that when we live and believe in Jesus, we've already passed from death to life.

A neighbor was invited to the coronation of the Queen of England. When she returned, I caught her radiance. Yet she was able to enter only as far as the vestibule of the throne room where the coronation took place. She saw the sights, she smelled the incense, she heard the voices, she experienced at first hand everything that was taking place. But she had not reached the peak experience, crossing the threshold into the presence of the queen. For us, as Christians, we await that final step.

But every stage of life we live with Jesus can be beautiful. Every step of the way provides glimpses of his light. I remember riding and walking up a mountain forty miles north of Tokyo. The views were splendid and every stage was more breathless than the one before. Yet the most captivating sights were reserved until I crossed the very top. In the sweep of the verdant valleys, hills, and trees I saw the ultimate.

When we live and believe in Jesus the power of death is broken. It's like living in a country that's been at war, but peace has been announced. There are still skirmishes on the fringes, but the war is over. The Lord Jesus has conquered. We can be at peace.

Yet the ultimate dream for Paul rises in his cry, "If by any means I might attain to the resurrection from among the dead." Only one reality grips his spirit. He wants desperately to share the world to come with Jesus. Like a mighty runner, he persists, in spite of everything, to reach his ultimate—life forever with God.

I can sense why King David sang in his immortal twenty-third Psalm, "Goodness and mercy shall *pursue* me all the days of my life." It's good all the way home. We sense oneness with a man who lived in a village next to mine when I was a college student. He came from Czechoslovakia. Though he had chosen America, his heart still clung to his homeland. He wrote what he called "The New World Symphony." In the middle of it are the haunting words that really defined his true homeland, "Goin' home, goin' home,

I'm just goin' home. It's not far, just close by, through an open door."

I've been with many saints who have seen heaven break for them when their longings have been fulfilled. I remember a young mother who said she saw angels waiting wall to wall. An old saint who raised himself up on his elbows prayed gently as he slipped away, "Lord Jesus, help me to your side." It's beautiful and it's real and it's all packaged and given to us by a fantastic person who said that he came from heaven to be our Savior, our Redeemer, our final bridge into the world to come. There we shall see him and not another, and our joy will be eternal. God bless you with this flaming hope.

THE PREACHER—Donald E. Zelle was born in Waverly, Iowa. He is a graduate of Wartburg College and Wartburg Seminary. He has served as pastor of Emmanuel, East Pittsburgh, Zion, Shawnee, Wisconsin, and St. Peter's in Dubuque, Iowa. At present he is pastor of First English Lutheran Church, Whitewater, Wisconsin.

THE OCCASION—Rodney was killed in a hunting accident. The fatal shot was fired by his brother, Craig. Rodney was a freshman in high school and had been confirmed six months before his death. His confirmation verse became the text for the sermon.

THE COMMENTS—The tragic circumstances made this a difficult sermon to preach. The minister here pulls no punches but goes right to the heart of the problem for the hearers, the family and the grieving brother. The use of the verse given in confirmation is particularly fitting here. A summary at the end might have helped the sermon. However, it is an excellent model for dealing with difficult situations.

Never Give Up

Keep alert and never give up. Ephesians 6:18b (TEV)

I address this sermon in three directions this afternoon, emphasizing the last words in verse 18, "keep alert and never give up."

First, to all who have gathered here to honor Rodney and support his family. It is important that we are here as we comfort this family by what we do and by what we say. Not everything that happens is the will of God. God did not take Rodney's life; a stray bullet did. Do not say that it was what God wanted! That would be unfair to God and to this family. We do not believe in a cruel God, but in a God who has given to mankind a large amount of freedom in which to live and move. God does not control every action and every event. With the practice of our freedom we are confronted with risks. There is room for accidents for which we feel responsible. That's the kind of world God made for us, and we would not want it to be any different. We would rather take the human risks than be God's robots.

One of the first reactions that several of you gave on

157

hearing about the accident was: "Those guns! I wish they never would have been invented." Or again: "I don't know why people go hunting; it's so dangerous!" It's easy for people who don't enjoy hunting to say that, yet there are many things that can be considered dangerous. Football can be dangerous. It's a sport based on contact, hard contact, and sometimes the harder, the better. Rodney loved football as you, his teammates, know. But does a person refuse to play football because it has an element of risk? Driving a car on our highways is dangerous, as we are especially reminded this Thanksgiving weekend, but do we get rid of our cars? Even eating and breathing can be dangerous!

The answer is not to withdraw from the world and protect ourselves inside a four-inch thick vault that has been fully sanitized. God wants us to participate in life, to enjoy life, and at all times to be as responsible as we can be, using our knowledge and abilities to care for the world, for our brothers and for ourselves.

Sometimes things go wrong in the world. Death is one of those things. A door slams shut, sometimes not gently as though blown by a breeze, but suddenly and with the sound of an explosion. Yet the Christian faith says that when that occurs, God opens another door, a door to another life. It is not easy to talk about the beginning of another life, even of an eternal life, when there was so much of this life left to live for Rodney, but if there ever is a time to hold on to the Christian hope of eternal life, this is the time. "For this reason, keep alert and never give up," our text says.

Second, a word to the family. The mind moves so

slowly at a time like this, like a glacier through a mountain pass. It is as though the drums that beat out the tempo of life have almost stopped, as we wait for an answer to the question, "Why?" The answer does not come, and our closest friends cannot find the proper words to explain it. Even those who have lived through similar tragedies in the past find that the question remains unanswered. That is because it can't be answered with the mind. We can only speak to it through the level of our emotions and the other, deeper level of faith.

Even God may not answer your questions, but he can comfort your hearts. God knows about grief. He lost his Son too, in death. He may not clear away all the rough spots in life, but he comes to walk that life with us. He comes to give strength and courage. God answers with a presence that supports our frail bodies and sets us on our way again. Maybe that is why the words of Psalm 23 came to you so soon after you heard the news: "Thou art with me; Thy rod and thy staff comfort me." God is with you, and he will continue to be.

Let me ask you to remember that Sunday morning here, last spring. Rodney was in this same place, at the foot of the altar. Here he told us what he believed. He confessed Jesus as his Lord. He promised to be faithful to God. That was his confirmation experience. A Bible verse was read at that time and given to him. Now I give it to all of you, his family, as a word for your life: "Ask for God's help. Pray on every occasion as the Spirit leads. For this reason keep alert, and never give up."

Third a word to Craig. You may, for the rest of your life, feel responsible for the death of your brother. People may even remind you about it. To help you, you will need to remember your brother's last words to you: "I know you didn't mean it." In the early part of the Bible, in the book of Genesis, there is the story of two brothers, Cain and Abel. It was not an accident that Abel was killed. Cain did it deliberately, and he carried a heavy load after that. He felt he was rejected by everyone. We hear him saying, "My punishment is greater than I can bear." Those may become your words, Craig, but remember this—God had mercy on him. He put a "mark" on Cain so that others would not take revenge on him. What that mark was we do not know, but we do know that it was a sign of God's mercy. God protected him and even blessed him.

God who had mercy on Cain who intentionally killed his brother, surely has mercy on you. He is your God. In Jesus he is your Savior, and he will bless you. You must go on believing that. "Never give up."